Miss Witherspoon
and
*Mrs. Bob Cratchit's Wild
Christmas Binge*

Works published by Grove Press by Christopher Durang:

The Marriage of Bette and Boo

Laughing Wild and *Baby with the Bathwater*

Christopher Durang Explains It All for You
(volume includes:
The Nature and Purpose of the Universe
'dentity Crisis
Titanic
The Actor's Nightmare
Sister Mary Ignatius Explains It All for You
Beyond Therapy)

Betty's Summer Vacation

Miss Witherspoon and *Mrs. Bob Cratchit's Wild Christmas Binge*

Miss Witherspoon
and
Mrs. Bob Cratchit's Wild
Christmas Binge

CHRISTOPHER DURANG

Grove Press
New York

Library of Congress Cataloging-in-Publication Data
Durang, Christopher, 1949–
  Miss Witherspoon ; and, Mrs. Bob Cratchit's wild Christmas binge : two plays / by Christopher Durang.
      p. cm.
  ISBN-10: 0-8021-4283-4
  ISBN-13: 978-0-8021-4283-2
  1. Suicide—Drama.   2. Reincarnation—Drama.   3. Dickens, Charles, 1812–1870 Christmas carol.   4. Scrooge, Ebenezer (Fictitious character)—Drama.   I. Durang, Christopher, 1949– Mrs. Bob Cratchit's wild Christmas binge.   II. Title.   III. Title: Mrs. Bob Cratchit's wild Christmas binge.
  PS3554.U666M588 2006
  812'.54—dc22   2006050739

Grove Press
an imprint of Grove/Atlantic, Inc.
841 Broadway
New York, NY 10003

Distributed by Publishers Group West

ww
06

CONTENTS

Miss Witherspoon
and
*Mrs. Bob Cratchit's Wild
Christmas Binge*

INTRODUCTION

Graham Greene was famous for making a distinction between his novels—he differentiated his psychological novels with conscience-ridden characters from what he called his "entertainments," which were his mystery books.

I've been wanting to adopt this same distinction in my own work between my satiric, dark comedy plays and my "entertainments," such as my parodies and what I might call my "friendly, silly" plays.

If you grant me this "satiric/dark comedy" works vs. "entertainments" distinction, this volume contains one of each.

Miss Witherspoon is not a satire, but it is a darkish comedy about a woman who commits suicide because she finds the world too scary and upsetting, and who is steadfastly refusing to reincarnate. It's actually not as harsh as some of my satires; it's also rather a fable; and in terms of tone, I like to say it's a "comedy to make you worry."

And *Mrs. Bob Cratchit's Wild Christmas Binge* is very much intended as an "entertainment." It's a playful reimagining of the Dickens classic *A Christmas Carol*, in which the usually long-suffering Mrs. Cratchit—who in the Dickens tale has almost no lines and sits in a chair knitting while poor Tiny Tim limps around the house—has in my version become imbued with a feisty rejection of all the endless suffering around her and proclaims her desire to go get drunk and then jump into the Thames River.

Thus, suicide seems to be a theme in both plays—which I didn't even think about until I wrote this introduction, partially because Mrs. Cratchit is so full of lively resistance to her given fate in life that her threats of ending her life are more emphatic railings than true intentions.

You know, she's like those lovable people in your life who say, "I swear you kids drive me crazy, I'm going out to the garage, shut the door, and turn on the ignition!" And then, depending on your age, you say, "Oh, Mummy, please don't kill yourself." And then she gives you food, and goes and takes a pill and a nap; and you eat the food while whimpering, and get very fat in later life.

Albert Camus wrote in his famous *The Myth of Sisyphus*: "There is but one truly serious philosophical question, and that is suicide." Do you know that quote? Do you like it? I always like to remind myself of that quote every morning, right before I decide whether to have coffee or to move to the Netherlands where I think they let doctors help you kill yourself. But then you have to use your passport, and the Bush administration might easily stop you at the airport, mistake you for a terrorist, and send you by rendition to a country where you will be tortured. So better stick with the coffee.

George W. Bush—or the Pigheaded President Who May Destroy the Planet and Cause the World to Come to an End, as he's nicknamed in my house—is not mentioned in my play *Miss Witherspoon*.

But in that title character's obsessive fears of terrorism, climate change from global warming, and her total distrust that anyone in charge of anything can be of any use to anybody, she and the play seem steeped in the fears and controversies that have dominated the reign of Bush II.

There's a lot about the afterlife in *Miss Witherspoon*.

Miss Witherspoon, though raised a Catholic (like me), finds herself in an Eastern afterlife with an Indian guide named Maryamma, and with lots of instructions about karma, learning life lessons, and preparing for her next incarnation back on earth. Miss Witherspoon explains over and over that she doesn't want to go back to earth, and struggles against it mightily, but in the end she . . . well, read it and see.

This volume could also be called the *Kristine Nielsen Volume*. Kristine is a brilliantly funny actress and in 1999 she won an Obie Award playing the happy and insanely oblivious Mrs. Siezmagraff in the New York premiere of my play *Betty's Summer Vacation*. So a year or so later, when I was writing *Mrs. Bob Cratchit's Wild Christmas Binge*, I was indeed thinking of Kristine for the leading role. And when it premiered at City Theatre in Pittsburgh, we were lucky enough to get her to play the part.

Kristine also was brilliant playing Miss Witherspoon, though she was not initially in my mind as I wrote the play. I had an image of an older woman—I kept thinking of the late, great actress Jessica Tandy, and I thought of her perennially worried look and her upswept worried hair in Alfred Hitchcock's movie *The Birds*. But when director Emily Mann and I considered how to cast the part, we wondered if there was any chance Ms. Tandy might come back to Earth, but her agent said no. Then we thought of the ever versatile Kristine, who beautifully embodied Miss Witherspoon's fears but who also added extra, unexpected colors with her comic buoyancy and invention.

Mrs. Bob Cratchit's Wild Christmas Binge ends happily, though in a perverse way. *Miss Witherspoon* ends hopefully, which I didn't expect it to as I was writing it.

I hope you enjoy the plays.

Christopher Durang
September 2006

MISS WITHERSPOON

Miss Witherspoon was commissioned by McCarter Theatre in Princeton, New Jersey, in 2004. It then was coproduced by McCarter and by Playwrights Horizons in New York City in the fall of 2005. It premiered at McCarter on September 9 and ran through October 16. There was a brief hiatus, and the same production and cast opened at Playwrights Horizons on November 11 and ran through January 1, 2006. The last two weeks were an extension of its originally planned run.

McCarter Theatre: Emily Mann, Artistic Director; Jeffrey Woodward, Managing Director; Mara Isaacs, Producing Director; David York, Production Manager; Janice Paran, Dramaturg.

Playwrights Horizons: Tim Sanford, Artistic Director; Leslie Marcus, Managing Director; William Russo, General Manager; Christopher Boll, Production Manager; Michael S. Borowski, Press Representative, The Publicity Office.

For both theaters: Set design was by David Korins; costume design by Jess Goldstein; lighting design by Jeff Croiter; sound design by Darren L. West. Casting was by Alaine Alldaffer, CSA, and James Calleri, CSA. Production stage manager was Alison Cote. Assistant stage manager was Christine Whalen.

Both productions were directed by Emily Mann. The cast of both productions was as follows:

Veronica	Kristine Nielsen
Maryamma	Mahira Kakkar
Mother 1 and Mother 2	Colleen Werthmann
Father 1, Father 2, Sleazy Man, Dog Owner, Soothing Voice, Wise Man	Jeremy Shamos
Teacher, Woman in a Hat	Linda Gravatt

Time: recent past, foreseeable future
Place: earth, and not earth

CHARACTERS

VERONICA

smart but worried woman, mid-forties to late fifties. Her nickname, we learn, is Miss Witherspoon.

MARYAMMA

a spirit guide in the netherworld. She may be any age, but she is intelligent, and has grace of movement and loveliness of spirit. She is also forceful when she needs to be. She wears a sari, and her ethnicity is Indian—that is, from India.

MOTHER 1

thirties, a new mother somewhere in Connecticut. Thrilled to have her new baby, sensible, nice.

FATHER 1

thirties, married to Mother 1. Also thrilled to have their first baby. He looks prosperous in a good suit, and probably works in the financial district. Sensible, nice.

MOTHER 2

thirties, drug addict much of the time; cranky to have a baby. Might dress in tank top and cutoffs. Not trying to be mean, but not fighting it either.

FATHER 2

Hell's Angel type, married to Mother 2. Drooping mustache, long hair, jean jacket, boots. Also a drug addict. Less consistently mean than Mother 2, but it's partially because he zones out a lot.

TEACHER

any age, but best forty to fifty-five. African American. A bit overworked, but a good teacher, intelligent, wants to help when she can. Though needs to set limits or she'll go crazy.

SLEAZY MAN
British guy named Stanley, hangs out in the playground selling drugs to children. Sleazy.

DOG OWNER
nice guy, thirties. Pretty average, has a girlfriend but they don't live together. Loves his dog.

SOOTHING VOICE
a soothing voice.

WOMAN IN A HAT
African American. A surprise visitor in the netherworld. Proud of her appearance, wears an impressive "going-to-church" hat. Sassy and pointed in her comments.

WISE MAN
another visitor in the netherworld. Dressed in long white robes, he is an articulate and somewhat powerful wizard.

In production, the following roles are doubled:
Mother 1 and Mother 2 are played by the same actress.
Teacher and Woman in a Hat are played by the same actress.
Father 1, Father 2, Sleazy Man, Dog Owner, Soothing Voice, and Wise Man are played by the same actor.

Lights up on VERONICA. *She is seated in a chair by a small telephone table. She is on the phone. She is in her late forties, maybe early fifties. Pleasant, in a nice skirt and blouse. Maybe once she worked in publishing. She has an undercurrent of sadness some of the time.*

VERONICA (*into phone*) Well that's just me. Kind of overwhelmed, kinda blue. That's how I am, I'm too old to change. Oh, just things. No I don't see him anymore. That's long gone. I'm really done with him. I'm kind of done with everything actually. (*listens, repeats back*) Look to the future. (*laughs*) Oh, I'm sorry, I thought you were making a joke. Oh you weren't. (*tries a bit to entertain this comment*) Look to the future. You mean, other men? Hope? I find it hard to get on the hope bandwagon, I always have. (*listens*) I've tried the antidepressants. They don't work. I'm antidepressant resistant. (*listens; irritated now*)

Well, no I haven't tried every single one. Listen, dear, I know I called you, and you're a dear person, but I think I shouldn't have called. I think I'm not in the mood to talk. I just need to go to the grocery store or something. Don't be offended, all right? (*listens*) Well, if you're going to be offended, then it just proves I can't get on with anybody, and that's kind of depressing to me. (*listens, very irritated*) Please stop talking about Zoloft! I've got to hang up. Please just understand who I am. I can't change. I don't want to change. Bye, dear, talk to you . . . sometime.

She hangs up; laughs. Frowns. Suddenly feels very sad, lost in thought. Throws off her thoughts, picks up pad and pencil that are on the telephone table.

Lights up on a larger area, which represents the outside, perhaps a small garden she keeps. Veronica leaves the chair area, and walks outside. The light is softer, there are the sounds of a few birds, it's restful. Veronica listens, and her whole body relaxes. She starts to write on the pad.

Eggs, butter, cheese. Bread, milk, frozen vegetables. Peas, carrots. String beans.

Suddenly a large "thing" drops from the sky, falling near where Veronica is. It seems to be metal and very heavy, and it makes a big clank when it falls. Or Sound creates the large clank. She screams.

AAAAAAAAAAAAAAAGGGGHHHHH!

Veronica stares at the object, alarmed and startled. Looks up to the sky. Moves a bit forward, tentatively. Doesn't know what to do. Goes back to her list.

Paper towels, tuna fish, mayonnaise.

A smaller object falls. Less scary, but nonetheless something falling. Veronica lets out a smaller yelp.

. . . aaaaaaa! Goodness. (*looks up again*)

A WOMAN IN A CHICKEN SUIT *comes running out.*

WOMAN IN CHICKEN SUIT   The sky is falling! The sky is falling!

VERONICA   What?

WOMAN IN CHICKEN SUIT   The sky is falling! It's falling! (*runs off in terror*)

VERONICA   What do you mean? (*looks worried, concerned*)

A third "thing" falls down on the other side of her. This one is quite big and thus quite scary.

AAAAAAAAAAAAAAAAAGGGGGHHHH!

She goes over to the object, looks at it. Looks upward again to see if there are more coming. She feels very afraid. She looks more closely at this third fallen object. Then she looks upward again.

Stop falling!

Suddenly a fourth object falls from the sky with a big thud.

And then a fifth object almost immediately afterward. Both terrorize her, but the fifth one frightens her even more—she wasn't expecting the fifth one so close after the fourth one. She throws her pad and pencil into the air, and runs off screaming.

AAAAAAAAAGHHHHH!!!

Lights dim to black. The sound of falling objects continues, intensifies. Scary, loud, disorienting.

Silence for a bit. The crashing of heavy objects from the sky seems to have stopped.

Quiet. There is the sound of waves for a bit, soft, but that dies down too.

SCENE 2

Lights come back on. Veronica is found standing in a pool of light. She speaks to the audience.

VERONICA Well, I'm dead. I committed suicide in the 1990s because of Skylab. Well not entirely, but it's as sensible an explanation as anything.

Most of you don't remember what Skylab was. . . . I seem to have had a disproportionate reaction to it, most people seemed to have sluffed it off.

Skylab was this American space station, it was thousands of tons of heavy metal, and it got put up into orbit over the earth sometime in the seventies.

Eventually the people on board abandoned it, and it was just floating up there; and you'd think the people who put it up there would have had a plan for how to get it back to earth again, but they didn't. Or the plan failed, or something; and in 1979 they announced that Skylab would eventually be falling from the sky in a little bit— this massive thing the size of a city block might come crashing down on your head as you stood in line at Bloomingdale's or sat by your suburban pool, or as you were crossing the George Washington Bridge, etc. etc.

Of course, STATISTICALLY the likelihood of Skylab hitting you on the head—or rather hitting a whole bunch of you on the head—statistically the odds were small.

But I can't live my life by statistics.

And the experts didn't think it through, I guess. Sure, let's put massive tonnage up in the sky, I'm sure it won't fall down. Sure, let's build nuclear power plants, I'm sure we'll figure out what to do with radioactive waste eventually.

Well you can start to see I have the kind of personality that might kill myself.

I mean throw in unhappy relationships and a kind of dark, depressive tinge to my psychology, and something like Skylab just sends me over the edge.

"I CAN'T LIVE IN A WORLD WHERE THERE IS SKYLAB!"—I sort of screamed this out in the airport as I was in some endless line waiting to go away to somewhere or other.

So I died sometime in the nineties. Obviously it was a *delayed* reaction to Skylab.

So I killed myself. Anger turned inward they say. But at least I got to miss 9/11.

If I couldn't stand Skylab, I definitely couldn't stand the sight of people jumping out of windows. And then letters with anthrax postmarked from Trenton. And in some quarters people danced in the streets in celebration. "Oh lots of people killed, yippee, yippee, yippee." God, I hate human beings. I'm glad I killed myself.

You know, in the afterlife I'm considered to have a bad attitude.

And apparently I'm slated to be reincarnated and come do this horrible thing again.

Why can't I just be left alone to fester and brood in my bodiless spirit state? Who says spirits have to be clear and light and happy? So what if my aura looks like some murky brown tweed suit? So what? Leave me alone, and I'll leave you alone.

Anyway, they tried to force me back onto earth in 2002 or so, and before I knew it my spirit was starting to reincarnate, but I put on some sort of spiritual otherworldly emergency brake system that I seem to have, and the whole process came to a grinding halt, and I simply REFUSED to reincarnate.

"What if I marry Rex Harrison again???" I said to them. Or maybe next time he'll be my mother and I'll get so frustrated maybe I'll go off the deep end and commit matricide. Or then there will be more Skylabs. And of course terrorism and anthrax and smallpox and monkey pox and a pox on everybody's houses. So no thank you.

Yes, I was married to Rex Harrison. He had several wives so you'll have to do research to figure out which one I was.

I really don't want to come back. I just find too much of it all too upsetting.

So I'm refusing to reincarnate, at least as much as I can. I didn't like being alive, I don't trust it. Plus, you know, if I can keep thwarting these attempts to reincarnate me, I'm not sure the earth is going to still be there, so if I stall long enough, my going back may become a moot point. (*looks at the audience, realizes what she said*) I'm sorry, am I depressing everyone? I'm depressing myself. Well pay no attention, I'm just a gloomy dead person, there's no accounting for my moods, I guess I was bipolar in life, and I still am out here in the afterlife.

Is there anything positive to leave you with? (*tries to think of something positive, has trouble thinking of anything; then tries this as a positive wish*) Well, good luck. I mean it sincerely. I guess life has always been scary—Hitler was scary, I was a child then; and we all expected to die from Russia and America aiming missiles at one another, and that didn't happen. So good luck—maybe it'll be all right. I hope it will. I just don't want to come back, but if I hear it all has worked out a bit better than we expected, well, I'll be glad. So long.

Lights dim on her. Maybe sounds of water. Then a light wind.

SCENE 3

Lights up. Veronica is seated on a chair, but is asleep, having a mild nightmare. She is in the bardo, a kind of netherworld.

Like images of heaven, this netherworld is filled with a beautiful blue— blue sky or blue nonrealistic background. The chair she sits in is in the shape of a traditional chair, but it might be see-through. You can see its shape, but sometimes she seems to be sitting on air.

Some quirks may be added to this netherworld. Pretty lanterns might be lowered from the sky, attached to what—who knows? Also if there are any other furniture or design elements, they should seem Eastern—from India, Thailand, etc.

Veronica is talking in her sleep, having a bad dream.

VERONICA   Look out, look out! Help! Help!

Enter an Indian woman—from India, that is, not Native American.

Her name is MARYAMMA. *She is dressed in a beautiful sari of rich, deep colors. She is attractive and smart, but also has a sharp edge to her.*

MARYAMMA   Come on now. Miss Witherspoon, wake up. Come on, wake up.

VERONICA   What? What? (*wakes*) Oh, it's you again. Leave me alone please.

MARYAMMA   You have a lot more lessons to learn, you're still focusing on your past life, or arguing with your ex-husband, you have a lot more lives to do, Miss Witherspoon.

VERONICA   My name isn't Miss Witherspoon.

MARYAMMA   Well we like to call you Miss Witherspoon. It's our nickname for your spirit. You're like some negative English woman in an Agatha Christie book who everybody finds bothersome. It's because of your brown tweed aura. You have a lot of aura cleansing to do in future lives, you know.

VERONICA   Aura cleansing. I don't know what that means.

MARYAMMA   My aura is light and airy and clear, Miss Witherspoon. Maybe after a few more lifetimes you'll be able to accurately see other people's auras.

VERONICA   I've explained as patiently as I can that I don't wish to go back to earth. Can't I just be left alone?

MARYAMMA   That's not how the netherworld works, Miss Witherspoon.

VERONICA   Is there someone above you I can speak to?

MARYAMMA   We don't think of people being above or below each other here. We're all part of the collective human soul.

VERONICA   Okay. But might I speak to some other member of the collective human soul, I don't feel you're understanding me.

MARYAMMA   Who do you want to speak to?

VERONICA   I don't know. Is Mahatma Gandhi here?

MARYAMMA   Yes he is. But your soul is in no way ready to meet him.

VERONICA   What's your name, I want to report you.

MARYAMMA   To whom would you report me?

VERONICA   Well, I don't know that now, but maybe later on it will become clear. What is your name?

MARYAMMA   I've told you before, I'm Maryamma.

VERONICA   Maryanna what?

MARYAMMA   I don't have a last name. And it's Mary*amma,* not Mary*anna.* The middle letters are not "n" as in Nancy, but "m" as in mellifluous . . . mary–yamma.

VERONICA   You know, I'm a Christian. I wasn't expecting some sort of Eastern religion person to greet me up here. I mean, I know a lot of American companies are hiring people in India to do phone work for them, but I wasn't expecting to find that in the afterlife as well.

MARYAMMA   There is no ethnicity in the bardo. That is just how you are choosing to see my spirit.

VERONICA   Really? Well I've imagined you in a very pretty sari.

MARYAMMA   Yes, and I appreciate it. But you know for the last thirty years of your life, you had no religion. And so your spirit is choosing to see me as an Indian woman because your soul is acknowledging reincarnation.

VERONICA   If there has to be an afterlife, I demand the pearly gates, and Saint Peter. And purgatory if I have to. And heaven so I can rest there. And I don't believe in hell.

MARYAMMA   Well that's very convenient for you. But even the people who see Saint Peter, reincarnate. Purgatory is actually reincarnation, that's why it lasts so long and has suffering in it. It's going back to earth and struggling over and over.

VERONICA   I don't believe you. You find some priest or minister to tell me that.

MARYAMMA   And sometimes Saint Peter looks like the traditional idea of him, robe and beard and all of that. And sometimes he looks like a Hawaiian man. And sometimes, in the last many years, he looks like E.T. or Yoda. The effect of movies on the collective unconscious.

VERONICA   I don't trust anything you're saying.

MARYAMMA   But you've had many lives already. You haven't just had one.

VERONICA   I don't believe you.

MARYAMMA   Yes. Remember 1692 in Massachusetts. Your sister was put to death as a witch. You knew it wasn't true, but you didn't speak up for her.

VERONICA   Well, of course. I would have been killed.

MARYAMMA   Oh so you remember?

VERONICA   No, I don't remember. I was speaking from common sense. If I had been there, what I would've thought. I've seen *The Crucible,* it was a terrible time. Doesn't mean I lived then.

MARYAMMA   Well you did. And you were a dance hall hostess in Wyoming in 1853. And you were a cloistered nun in 1497 in Düsseldorf.

VERONICA   Düsseldorf? I don't believe you. And I certainly remember nothing.

MARYAMMA   You're just stubborn. Think back. You can remember all the other lives up here in the bardo, when you want to. It's back on earth you can't remember them, or just remember little pieces of them. Remember the song "Where or When"?

VERONICA   Yes, it was very pretty, but it was about a small hotel, it wasn't about reincarnation.

MARYAMMA   You're confusing it with "There's a Small Hotel." "Where or When" was indeed about reincarnation.
(sings)
It seems we've stood and talked like this before
We looked at each other in the same way then
But I can't remember where or when. . . .

VERONICA   That's about forgetful lovers, it's not about reincarnation.

MARYAMMA   It IS about reincarnation.

VERONICA   I know Mary Rodgers, the daughter of Richard Rodgers, and I'm going to ask her to write you a letter explaining "Where or When" to you.

MARYAMMA   There's no way a letter can be delivered in the bardo.

VERONICA   You keep saying the bardo, but you don't say what you mean. What is the bardo?

MARYAMMA   It's where you are now. It's a stopping-off place where you can choose your next life, and then drink from the Lake of Forgetfulness before you return to the earth plane again.

VERONICA Drink from the Lake of Forgetfulness. You're some terrible dream I'm having. If this is the afterlife, I demand to see Saint Peter. And not the E.T. one either.

MARYAMMA You don't really qualify as a Christian. In your last life you stopped believing in it early on, so demanding to go to Christian heaven is not your right after this past lifetime.

VERONICA Ah, so there is a Christian heaven?

MARYAMMA Yes. For those who believe in it, there is. And there's a pet heaven. And a Muslim heaven. And a Jewish heaven which, since they don't believe in an afterlife, is kind of like prolonged general anesthesia.

VERONICA Oh I want that one! Send me to that one.

MARYAMMA Your soul automatically chooses the image of heaven it wishes to see. You may be telling me you want to see Saint Peter, but your soul has chosen that you see me and I need to get you to reincarnate. And none of those funny shenanigans about stopping it from happening this time.

VERONICA It's scary down there, and it's painful, and if you want me to learn some lesson or other, well give me a book and I'll read it. But I don't want to go back there.

MARYAMMA It's not your choice. All souls must keep reincarnating until they reach true wisdom, at which point they sometimes go back to guide others—like Gandhi did—or sometimes they reach nirvana, and their spirit permeates and uplifts the collective unconscious.

VERONICA Just leave me at this level, I'm not harming anybody, just let me rest here in the . . . bardo.

MARYAMMA I've told you that cannot be your choice.

VERONICA Well I've stopped it several times so far, haven't I?

MARYAMMA That's true. We're all a little confused by that. The force of your will has been creating a little glitch up here, and the reincarnation process keeps aborting itself with you. We've asked Gandalf to look into that so that your next reincarnation actually occurs.

VERONICA Gandalf? Isn't he a fictional figure from *The Lord of the Rings*?

MARYAMMA Yes, there is the fictional character Gandalf. But he in turn was based on a real person of great wisdom also named Gandalf, who's lived many centuries, and who's very involved with helping souls to continue their evolution in the bardo and back on earth.

VERONICA I wonder if I'm in a coma and I'm dreaming you.

MARYAMMA Life is the dream.

VERONICA Yes, yes, I've heard that before. It's very confusing. I don't wish to play these games. I want that Jewish heaven which is like general anesthesia. I want to be put out like a light.

MARYAMMA You only get that when your soul believes in no afterlife. But even then it's an illusion . . . you are in that blank state for a while, but after a bit, your soul still reincarnates, and eventually most souls on earth begin to believe in some sort of afterlife. After all, as Thornton Wilder said, everybody knows in their bones that something is eternal.

VERONICA I like Thornton Wilder. Is he here?

MARYAMMA Yes, but he's presently reincarnated.

VERONICA Really? As who?

MARYAMMA As Arianna Huffington.

VERONICA I don't believe Thornton Wilder is Arianna Huffington.

MARYAMMA   No, I was kidding. Thornton Wilder has achieved nirvana, and is no longer reincarnating, but his soul sends out wonderful vibrations throughout the entire universe.

VERONICA   There's an Indian restaurant on West Fifty-ninth Street that overlooks Central Park South, and it's called Nirvana.

MARYAMMA   And your point is?

VERONICA   No point, I guess. I'm feeling tired, my brain hurts. Can I be allowed to sleep a little more?

MARYAMMA   Yes, your spirit depletes quickly, you need to achieve more stamina.

VERONICA   Easier said than done, Maryamma Nirvana-head. Oh, gosh, my eyes are so heavy.

She falls asleep.

Maryamma exits quietly, wanting her to sleep.

Lights dim and perhaps change color. We hear the sound of wind whooshing.

A spotlight comes up on Veronica. It's bright and the rest of the stage is dim or a vastly different color. It's like there's a wind machine underneath her . . . her clothes are being blown strongly, and hair. There might be a light from underneath her too . . . it's like she's flying through space and time back to earth.

She stays seated in her chair, holding on for dear life, as her body and especially legs are being drawn to the side, into some vortex that is the entry back to a life on earth.

Note: Most of this should be done by the actress herself, with body movements.

Oh God, it's happening again. No thank you. I don't want to go. I'm not going. (*makes facial grimaces, resisting being pulled down to earth*) Stop it now. Hell no, I won't go! Hey hey, LBJ, how many kids did you kill today? God, what am I talking about? Stop it! I won't go back! Stop it!

The spotlight goes out on Veronica. The whooshing sound stops. There is the sound of a baby crying. It's pretty dim onstage.

Scene 4

Then lights up. A nursery. Veronica is in a bassinet with a baby bonnet on her head. She looks ahead with a baby's innocent, uncertain look. Her face looks its correct age, of course, but she is now a curious, normally happy baby.

Looking fondly at the baby in the bassinet is the MOTHER. She is dressed tastefully and is clearly middle to upper middle class. Mother is probably thirties, pleasant, happy to have a baby.

Note: This is an "on earth" setting, but it should not take up the whole stage space, especially if you have a normal-sized theater. It should either be a small set of a bedroom that lives within the larger bardo set, or it could perhaps be done with just a few pieces of furniture and lighting. For this scene the bassinet is especially important.

MOTHER   Hello, darling. Hello there. Yes. It's Mommy. Hello. Good morning. How did precious sleep?

VERONICA   Ga ga. Goo goo. Ma-ma-ma! Ma-ma-ma!

MOTHER   Yes, "Mama!"

Note: The actress playing Veronica should not attempt to do "realistic baby sounds." She should do the "ga ga, goo goo" sounds as if that is how babies indeed speak at that age. A bit like having an actor playing a dog say "woof, woof," rather than imitating a real bark. And the "baby lines" should indeed sound a bit babyish, and should be said quickly.

VERONICA   Ma-ma-ma! Ma-ma-ma!

MOTHER   One less syllable, dear. Ma-ma.

VERONICA   Ma-ma-ma! Ma-ma-ma! *(to herself; her adult voice)* Oh God, I'm a baby again. Oh Lord, no I can't go through this again, it's endless.

MOTHER   What, dear?

VERONICA (*baby talk sounds*)   Google, google.

MOTHER   Yes, Google, that's a search engine. Oh, David, she's very chatty this morning. She almost said "Mama."

Enter DAVID, the FATHER. Thirties. He's in a suit, dressed for work. Also pleasant, a bit prosperous. Also happy to have a baby.

FATHER   Talkative, is she? Good morning, sweet pea.

VERONICA   Goo goo, la la la la.

FATHER   That's right, darling, very good. What a beautiful baby.

Sound of dog barking, then growling.

MOTHER   Oh David, don't let Fido in here.

VERONICA (*her adult voice, to herself*)   "Fido"—give me a break. (*calls out upward, adult voice still*) Someone get me out of here!

MOTHER   Oh, she seems restless. Are you restless, darling?

VERONICA (*assenting to question*)   Ga ga ga! Ma-ma.

MOTHER   Oh she said "Ma-ma." Yes, darling. I'm Ma-ma.

Sound of dog growling. The actors playing Mother and Father can play that the dog has entered the room, pretend he's present.

David, take Fido out. I think he's jealous of the baby.

FATHER   He's just not used to her yet. He'll learn to accept her.

MOTHER   Well he doesn't usually show his teeth, I don't like that.

VERONICA (*with a glint; baby voice, but awfully articulate*)   Doggie! Like doggie! Let him stay!

Mother and Father are speechless.

MOTHER   Good God, did you hear that? She formed real sentences.

FATHER   Did we imagine it?

MOTHER   I don't think so. Darling, did you say doggie? Doggie?

VERONICA (*trying to get them off track*)   Googie. Ga ga.

MOTHER   Maybe she said googie and it sounded like doggie.

FATHER   That must have been it. Is that what you said, little Miss Witherspoon?

Veronica looks startled.

MOTHER   David, what did you call her?

FATHER   I'm not certain. It was just an impulse. You know that nursery rhyme, whither the spoon goes, whither the fork.

MOTHER   Whither the spoon? I've never heard that nursery rhyme.

FATHER   No, neither have I, come to think of it.

Dog growls again.

Fido, no!

Slaps dog's nose, seemingly.

MOTHER   Well don't hit the dog, David. Just leave him outside.

FATHER   All right. Out in the hallway, Fido. Go find your ball. Go on.

Dog apparently leaves; Father turns back to Mother.

So you don't want to call her Miss Witherspoon?

MOTHER   What? Are you insane?

FATHER   Well you choose the name, I'm clearly out of my league. Goodbye, sweet pea, see you tonight. Daddy's off to business.

MOTHER   Oh, darling, I'll see you to the car. There are some things I want you to pick up on your way home.

Mother and Father leave. Veronica looks bored.

VERONICA   Ga ga ga. Moooooo. La la la. (*adult voice*) Oh God, I have to relearn language. It takes so long. Why am I remembering everything?

Dog growls. Dog has apparently come back in the room. Veronica looks very interested.

Oh. Oh, yes.

Combination of baby and adult voice; gets glint of purpose.

Ga ga, here, doggie. Here, doggie. Come here, Fido. I'm taking your place in the house. Come here. Here, doggie.

More growling.

Oh yes, big teeth. Very big teeth. Here, doggie, come here, come here.

Veronica makes her neck available to the dog. Barking sounds continue.

Blackout.

Terrible dog barking sounds in the dark. Wind whooshing, ocean breaking on the waves—and then boom!

SCENE 5

Lights back on, Veronica arrives back in the bardo.

VERONICA   I'm back, I'm back, hooray, hooray!

Maryamma comes rushing in, angry.

MARYAMMA   What did you just do?

VERONICA   I'm back!

MARYAMMA   Did you just commit suicide at two weeks old???

VERONICA   It wasn't my fault. You sent me where there was a vicious dog.

MARYAMMA Yes, but you chose . . . Oh forget it, that was a wasted lifetime. And that poor couple are going to suffer and have guilt, and try to make it up with the next child who's going to be spoiled and will take no responsibility for anything and then will get drunk at age sixteen and drive a car without a license and kill two people—you see what you've done?

VERONICA I didn't do it. If that's how they behave, that's how they behave, it's not my fault.

MARYAMMA Your aura is worse than before.

VERONICA Look, I was thinking. I don't want Saint Peter. I want to go to the Jewish heaven which is like general anesthesia. Can you arrange that please?

MARYAMMA This isn't a spa.

VERONICA Not only do I not like life on earth, I realize I don't like to be conscious. I don't want to be here talking to you. I would consider it a wonderful favor if you could arrange for me to be put under.

MARYAMMA The general anesthesia afterlife is just what happens to the people who don't believe in an afterlife. And you can't just choose the Jewish heaven. Plus I sort of misspoke. It's not only Jewish people. It's also people like Jean-Paul Sartre and Camus. You know, people who don't believe in an afterlife.

VERONICA I want blankness, I want nothing.

MARYAMMA Between grief and nothing, I'd choose grief, William Faulkner wrote. Later Jean-Paul Belmondo took the same quote in the movie *Breathless* and said, "I'd choose nothing."

VERONICA (*brief pause*) Why are you telling me this?

MARYAMMA What you said just made me think of it, that's all. You're choosing nothing. It's a negative choice, nothing. People who go to a restaurant and order nothing, don't eat. Their bodies don't get nourishment. Nothing is as nothing does.

VERONICA   I don't remember those lines in *Breathless*.

MARYAMMA   Oh you saw the film?

VERONICA   I didn't see the Godard version. I saw the Richard Gere remake on HBO one night.

MARYAMMA   I hate when they make remakes of classic films. It's terrible. It's like when someone says a beautiful sentence, and then some jerk later on comes and says, "Let me paraphrase that for you."

VERONICA   Yes, Rex always hated remakes too. Gosh even saying his name makes me angry. Is there a hell and can you check if he's there?

MARYAMMA   What do you have against Rex Harrison?

VERONICA   I told you, I was married to him. And he wasn't very nice.

MARYAMMA   I explained before, you were married to the soul of Rex Harrison but not when he was Rex Harrison. He had similarities, but he was a coal miner in 1876. In your last life you kept recognizing him when you'd see the actor Rex Harrison, but you were actually recognizing your husband from 1876, not the person who won the oscar for *My Fair Lady*.

VERONICA   What are you talking about? I remember going to the Oscars with Rex Harrison.

MARYAMMA   You're blurring memories, dreams, and fantasies. It's partially that brown tweed aura of yours, thoughts get stuck in it.

VERONICA   I thought you said we could remember our past lives up here.

MARYAMMA   I did. But people are all on different levels of development, and because of your continuing negative choices, your level of development is fairly messed up.

VERONICA   You're very critical, and you're not very encouraging. I'd like you to go away now, and if I can't be under general anesthesia, then I'd just like to sit and stare and try to think nothing for a while.

Veronica sits in her chair, hoping to end the conversation and to zone out for a while.

MARYAMMA   Well two years have gone by since we started this conversation. . . .

VERONICA   What?

MARYAMMA   So it's time for you to reincarnate again.

VERONICA   It can't be. I just got here.

MARYAMMA   Goodbye.

Maryamma exits.

Whooshing sounds again. Veronica is suddenly in that same place in her chair—the air whooshing up at her hair, the light from below, sounds of rushing through air, being sucked downward. Once again her legs are being pulled by some force, back down to earth.

Lights dim or almost go to black on Veronica.

SCENE 6

Lights up come up on a second MOTHER *and* FATHER.

They are played by the same actors who played the previous mother and father, but they look and seem very different.

Mother 2 and Father 2 are of a lower social class. Indeed they are trailer trash.

Mother 2 has a cigarette dangling, and coughs a lot. Father 2 is a Hell's Angel type. Long hair, dirty T-shirt. Leather jacket probably.

Note: Let's avoid making them sound Southern. Think instead of angry "super size" people in Ohio, or upstate New York. Maybe Monticello,

New York. And they can also be angry thin people, too. Just not Southern.

If there's a setting, it should look run-down and depressing.

Veronica once again is a baby, and is in a new bassinet, and is wearing a dirty baby's cap. The bassinet may not be a regular bassinet. It may be a tin washing tub, or something like that.

MOTHER 2 Hey, baby. Gee, it's kind of a fat baby, isn't it?

FATHER 2 Yeah, it's gonna have your fat ass.

MOTHER 2 Shut up. It's gonna have your greasy hair and damaged brain cells.

FATHER 2 Yeah, well I had fun damaging them.

MOTHER 2 Good for you. Why isn't the baby responding? Is it dead? Are you dead. (*yells*) HEY, BABY! Hey, fat ass! You dead?

Veronica has been looking around, kind of worried, starting to be alarmed. Now she expresses herself:

VERONICA Waaaaaaaaaaaaaaa! Waaaaaaaaaaaaaaaaaaa! (*cries are those of an unhappy baby; momentarily she switches to adult self, and looks around her, horrified*) Oh my God! Where am I? Oh Lord. (*back to crying*) Waaaaaaaaaaaaaa!

MOTHER 2 Shut up! God, it's so ugly when it cries. (*to the baby*) You're ugly!

VERONICA (*adult for a sec*) Oh, God, what is this? Do they have a dog, I wonder? (*baby again*) Waaaaaaaaaaaaa!

MOTHER 2 Shut up! (*to husband*) Where's Spot the wonder dog, I want him to meet baby.

VERONICA (*as adult*) Oh good! (*as baby, happy*) Ga ga, ga ga.

FATHER 2 I shot the dog this morning.

Veronica looks a bit appalled, as well as worried—how does she get out of here?

MOTHER 2   Oh so that's what that noise was. I thought you farted. (*laughs at her joke, but then:*) How come you shot the dog?

FATHER 2   It annoyed me.

VERONICA (*adult*)   Oh Lord. How do I get out of this? (*baby*) Waaaaaaaaaaaaa!

MOTHER 2   God, it's such a noisy baby. Do you think it's defective?

FATHER 2   Well it came out your fat ass, it's bound to be defective.

MOTHER 2   I need a joint. Do you think the baby can inhale? Maybe that'll stop it from crying? You want some pot, baby? That shut you up?

VERONICA (*adult, thinking, worried*)   No dog. No escape. Pot. Okay. (*baby again; nods*) Ahhh, ga ga.

Lights dim down briefly, come back up. To signify time passing.

·

Scene 7

Veronica is now very much a five-year-old girl. Kind of normal, vulnerable. But also unhappy, a little "dead." She doesn't seem to have access to her adult "soul self" anymore. She is no longer in the tub/bassinet, she's seated on a chair.

Mother 2 and Father 2 are still there, though it's five years later for them too. Father 2 seems out of it.

MOTHER 2   Hey, Ginny. You want another piece of pie?

VERONICA   Okay.

MOTHER 2   Wipe your mouth, you look like a pig.

VERONICA   Am I pretty?

MOTHER 2   Didn't I just call you a pig?

VERONICA   Yes.

MOTHER 2   So don't ask dumb questions.

VERONICA   I'm hungry.

MOTHER 2   So eat another piece of pie, I told you to. You're so fat already, it don't matter what you eat.

VERONICA   Will I ever go to school?

MOTHER 2   Stop asking about school. We're doin' home schooling with you, so you can learn real values. (*to Father 2*) You're awful quiet today.

FATHER 2   That's because I'm overdosing. (*falls down dead*)

MOTHER 2   Oh fuck. You jerk. Leaving me alone. Oh fuck. I need to shoot up. Finish your pie, Ginny.

VERONICA (*worried*)   Don't take an overdose.

MOTHER 2   I know what I'm doin'. Give me ten minutes to get high first, and then call an ambulance for him. And finish your pie. (*exits, muttering*) Fuckin' useless husband.

Veronica/GINNY looks around kind of lost.

VERONICA   Dad? You dead? I'm gonna call the ambulance, but Mom said to wait ten minutes, she wants to get high. (*looks around, more sense of panic, being lost*) Maybe I better have two pieces of pie.

Lights dim.

Noise, various noises—trucks, horns, trucks backing up beep-beep-beep. They're not necessarily in a city—though they may be. It's just there are noises, unpleasant ones. It's "time passing" noises. The noises lessen, and we hear voices in the dark.

MOTHER 2 (*voice*) What's seven times seven?

GINNY (*voice*) I don't know.

MOTHER 2 Well, think, idiot.

GINNY Fifty-six.

MOTHER 2 No!

Slap sound.

GINNY Ow!

MOTHER 2 Forty-nine, forty-nine . . . I give up, two years of home schooling is killin' me, you're going to public school, how do ya like that?

GINNY I'd like it fine.

Slap sound.

Ow!

MOTHER 2 Don't be fresh!

GINNY I wasn't.

Sound of a big slap.

OW!

Scene 8

A schoolroom.

Lights up on a TEACHER. She sits at a desk. There are two chairs by the desk.

The Teacher is a black woman, sympathetic, intelligent.

Mother 2 and Veronica/Ginny come in.

TEACHER   Ah, you must be Mrs. Fortunata. I'm afraid I'm running late, I can't give you as much time as I planned, the previous student had a nosebleed.

MOTHER 2 (*curious*)   Did ya punch him?

TEACHER (*slightly taken aback*)   No, it was just a nosebleed. But I hadn't allotted time for it, and now I've fallen behind. Sorry. (*realizes she hasn't said hi to Ginny*) Hello, Virginia, how are you today?

Ginny shrugs. Teacher speaks to Mother 2.

And thank you so much for coming.

MOTHER 2   Sure.

TEACHER   Mrs. Fortunata, I wanted to talk to you because Virginia seems kind of lost in school.

MOTHER 2 (*to Veronica/Ginny, immediately "at" her*)   What did I tell you about being lost? Huh? What did I say?

VERONICA   I don't know. You say a lot of things.

MOTHER 2   Well pay attention to what I say. (*to teacher*) She don't listen to what I say.

TEACHER (*slightly considers correcting her grammar, decides not to*) Uh-huh. Well she's not learning at the seventh-grade level.

MOTHER 2 (*looking at Ginny during the above comment*)   Ginny, your mind is wandering, stop it.

Mother 2 snaps her fingers. Veronica looks over at her mother, blankly.

Pay attention! (*pinches Veronica/Ginny*)

VERONICA   Ow!

MOTHER 2 (*to teacher*)   Go ahead. You have about six seconds she'll keep listening.

TEACHER (*bit disoriented by the mother*)   Okay. As I said, I'm concerned about Virginia. She's failing most of her subjects.

MOTHER 2 (*to Ginny*) Why can't you learn anything? You're useless.

She swats her on the head.

TEACHER Uh . . . no hitting please. Lord, I don't have time to solve this.

MOTHER 2 What?

TEACHER Nothing. Just we have a "no hitting" policy.

MOTHER 2 I don't believe that socialist crap you can't hit your kids. (*to Veronica*) You don't do better in school, and I'm yankin' you outta here, and we're doin' home schooling again. How'd you like that?

VERONICA You don't know nothin'.

MOTHER 2 You have respect for your mother, you fat pig. (*to teacher*) You see what I have to go through with her?

VERONICA You're right, I'm useless.

MOTHER 2 (*makes a fist*) How'd you like a bloody nose, you keep talkin' back to me?

TEACHER STOP IT, STOP IT!

MOTHER 2 What?

TEACHER This is not acceptable behavior.

MOTHER 2 What isn't?

TEACHER Mrs. Fortunata, I'd like to speak to you without Virginia being here for a moment.

MOTHER 2 Anything you wanna say to me, just say it. She can hear it.

TEACHER (*pause, decides to go ahead*) Mrs. Fortunata, I'm . . . upset how you speak to your daughter.

MOTHER 2   I'm the mother, I gotta correct her. She's constantly failing, what, I'm supposed to praise her for that? (*to Ginny, with a mocking voice*) Oh, Ginny, you're so good! You're dumb and you're fat, but it's fun to watch you eat twenty doughnuts at a time, and maybe you can grow up and be a elephant in the circus. Ginny's great, Ginny's great!

VERONICA   I want to take an overdose like Daddy did.

MOTHER 2   You're too young for hard drugs.

TEACHER   STOP IT, STOP IT!

MOTHER 2   Stop telling me to stop it. You stop it!

TEACHER   Virginia can't survive if you tell her she's worthless.

MOTHER 2 (*to Ginny*)   Did I call you worthless?

VERONICA   You did yesterday!

MOTHER 2   I'm not talking about yesterday.

TEACHER   STOP! Look, I'm not a psychologist, but maybe the school can come up with money to send you both for family counseling. I'm sorry, I have to move on to the next patient now . . . I mean parent.

MOTHER 2 (*fed up, gets up to go*)   Counseling! You go to counseling, I'm going to the liquor store. Come on, Ginny, let's get you an ice cream cone.

Mother 2 takes Veronica/Ginny off. The Teacher looks exhausted, she holds her head in her hands, or shudders, or does something to deal with bad energy.

TEACHER   Oy.

Lights dim as the Teacher exits.

SCENE 9

Sounds of a playground.

A SLEAZY MAN *enters into the playground. Played by same actor who was Father 1 and Father 2. Mustache, lanky, loose. Wears black jeans, black T-shirt, maybe leather jacket. Sleazy, but a bit sexy too.*

SLEAZY MAN (*has a British accent of some sort; speaks to a child who is presumably walking by*)   Hey, luv. Want some smoke? Special sale today, come on, honey.

Sleazy man looks disappointed, looks after where the child presumably exited.

Enter Veronica/Ginny. Drinking a diet soda.

Hey, Ginny.

VERONICA   Hello, Stanley.

SLEAZY MAN   You got that "wantin' it" look in your eye. I told you, hon, you gotta have money. I'm not a charity organization.

VERONICA   I got money today. For my birthday.

SLEAZY MAN   Oh, how old are you?

VERONICA   I'm thirteen.

SLEAZY MAN   That's a good age. Soon you can have your own baby and ruin her life. That's a good revenge, huh?

VERONICA   Where in England are you from?

SLEAZY MAN   Liverpool.

VERONICA   I like English accents. In school they showed us this movie from years and years ago called *My Fair Lady,* and Rex Harrison taught Audrey Hepburn how to talk good. (*corrects herself*) To talk well.

SLEAZY MAN   Yeah, I saw that once. Very long movie.

VERONICA   You remind me of Rex Harrison somehow.

SLEAZY MAN   Do I? It must be me charm. So how much money you got today?

VERONICA Fifty.

SLEAZY MAN Oh, you're doing well.

VERONICA I got ten for my birthday, and I got forty more nobody knows about.

SLEAZY MAN Atta girl. I can sell you a good party for fifty.

VERONICA Do you have some of those pills you talked about? That make you spacey and happy?

SLEAZY MAN I sure do, sweet cakes. You can have three for fifty.

VERONICA Three? (*seems a small number to her*)

SLEAZY MAN They're really good.

VERONICA Okay.

SLEAZY MAN But spread 'em out, don't take 'em all at once or you won't wake up.

VERONICA Three would do that?

SLEAZY MAN If you don't spread 'em out.

VERONICA All right, I'll spread 'em out.

She hands him the money; he gives her a little packet, pretending he's not doing a transaction, looking around or something.

SLEAZY MAN (*sings to himself, while they do the above exchange*)
London Bridge is falling down,
Falling down, falling down,
London Bridge is . . .

Jumps to end of melody.

. . . my fair lady.

Done with selling, ready to move on.

Well you have a nice party, Virginia.

VERONICA   Thanks.

Sleazy Man exits.

Veronica looks around, takes a pill, drinks from diet soda. A thought now crosses her mind. Makes a decision.

Takes a second pill. Pauses. Takes a third pill.

Happy birthday, Virginia.

Lights dim. Emergency sounds, ambulance, flashing lights.

Then whooshing noise, then wind, then ocean sounds. Final whoosh and—

SCENE 10

Veronica is back in the bardo. She's a bit shell-shocked.

VERONICA   Oh God.

Enter Maryamma.

MARYAMMA *(disapproving, maybe angry)*   I see you're back.

VERONICA   That was horrible! How could you do that to me? I had no chance in that situation, that was pure hell.

MARYAMMA   No one did it to you, Miss Witherspoon. Your soul makes the choice of the life that will teach you the lesson you need to learn.

VERONICA   What lesson was that? Life is hell? I already knew that.

MARYAMMA   I can't explain it to you fully. It's not punishment, but it's karma, we have to learn. And you keep killing yourself, that doesn't make good karma. You don't get ahead with suicide.

VERONICA   Next time you try to reincarnate me, I'm going to be able to stop it again. I know I will.

MARYAMMA   Well, you're very willful. We've all noted it.

VERONICA I mean what else could I have done with that life?

MARYAMMA I don't know. . . . You could have tried to befriend the teacher.

VERONICA What good would that have done?

MARYAMMA (*sharp*) Well, I don't know. You didn't try it.

VERONICA I was depressed. I was hyperglycemic. I was on various drugs.

MARYAMMA I admit. It was a very difficult life. For your next life . . .

VERONICA Don't finish that sentence. I need to recuperate after that life. (*getting upset*) Did you ever see *Stop the World I Want to Get Off*? That musical with Anthony Newley, I think Rex and I saw it together—and I was married to him, don't tell me I knew him when he was a coal miner in some previous century—anyway that musical's title was prescient, wasn't it? Who thought Anthony Newley knew anything? Oddest singer I ever heard, but he was on to something. Stop the world, stop the bardo, I want off. Don't send me back for more suffering. What's the matter with you?

MARYAMMA (*softer, sympathetic to her upset*) Suffering and life are mysteries, Miss Witherspoon. We can't choose to escape from them. They are inescapable.

VERONICA (*pause; stares at her; cold*) May I see Saint Peter please?

MARYAMMA (*uncertain pause; then:*) I'll see what I can do.

Maryamma exits.

VERONICA (*calling after her*) And I don't want him to look like E.T. either! I want him in a beard and a staff and a robe. I don't want any "modern interpretations" of him, for God's sake. (*is pent-up, upset; shakes her arms and whole body, as if to "shake off" the experience of the last life; looks out to the audience*) Well I think I made a point with her. All this repeating of life after life. Christianity

34

taught me one life, one roll of the dice, and it's heaven, hell, or purgatory, but it's clear and simple. And it's over.

So Saint Peter can set this straight, I hope. Because for most of my lives I was a Christian, so I am expecting heaven or purgatory.

I don't want hell, of course, but after all I wasn't Hitler, I may have my quirks, but really purgatory should be the appropriate place for me, I believe. That's just that place where you can't see God for eons and eons 'cause you weren't perfect, and I don't know it may be unpleasant, but I don't think they torture you there or anything. Maybe you only eat bread or water. Maybe it's like prison. But not Spanish Inquisition prison—that would be more like hell—it's just "prison" prison.

Here I am longing for purgatory. Strange, I actually thought the afterlife would be nothing . . . you know, like life is a television set with horrible things on it, but then you die and the television set is just unplugged. Nothing going in, nothing going out. I want to be unplugged!

I can't stand the idea that this just goes on forever. Or if not forever, until you learn a hundred and two fucking lessons. Who came up with that idea? The American Federation of Teachers?

Whoosh sound begins. She holds on to her chair.

Oh my God, another life is starting. NO! I'm waiting to see Saint Peter, I'm not available for another life right now. I'm on hold. I can't go, I won't go.

Whoosh stops.

Good. My force of will is working again.

Whoosh starts again.

AAAAAAgggggghhhhh! NO NO NO NO NO NO NO NO!

Whoosh stops again.

Thank God.

I think I did stop it. Just like those other times. My little brake system. Stubbornness is a wonderful thing.

Now if only my brain will let up. I don't see why Jewish people and Jean-Paul Sartre get to be in some general anesthesia state, and I get to remember things and fret and worry, and my brain goes on and on, and I just don't like it. It's not fair. (*thinking of other people who get this state*) Albert Camus, Simone Signoret probably.

How am I to learn "lessons" anyway if they don't tell me what they are, and if I can't really remember the past lives when I'm down there. And what lessons am I supposed to learn? (*calling*) Maryamma! I'm still waiting for Saint Peter. Are you bringing him? I really am a Christian. Tell him that!

(*to self or audience*) Though that's not really true. I have a problem with the crucifixion. I didn't used to, I didn't used to think about it . . . but the meaning of it has become . . . "odd" to me.

I mean, it starts with Adam and Eve, eating the apple . . . which is disobedient, and God goes ballistic—creates death and suffering, and punishes everybody by giving them original sin, which keeps them out of heaven forever.

But after a while God cools down a bit. And now He feels bad no one can get into heaven. So then He goes, "I know, I know, I'll send down my only son to be tortured and die." And we are taught that somehow this sacrifice will expiate our sins. "Atone for."

So when I was seven, I believed that.

But when I was twenty-seven, I got to thinking about sacrifice, and how in the Old Testament God seems to require animal sacrifices . . . "Kill an animal for me, so I know you love me." Which seems a bit odd, why does He find it pleasing that we kill animals for him?

And then He almost moved up to human sacrifice when He told Abraham to kill His son Isaac . . . but then God relented and said, "No, no—you can just kill an animal for me, I was testing you."

But then later God Himself does what He stopped Abraham from doing—He lets His only begotten Son die so that our sins can be atoned for.

But what about forgiveness without killing an animal? Or a person? Or your son? I don't understand it, it doesn't make sense.

Imagine if your child did something really, really bad, and you said, "Okay I'm going to forgive you, but we're going to have to kill your sister first."

I mean, do you understand psychologically what my problem is with the crucifixion?

I bet this isn't a popular thought I'm expressing, but that's how it strikes me now. And why I can't really call myself a Christian. (*frowns, realizes:*) Oh except I'm waiting for Saint Peter. No, I do believe in the crucifixion. I believe it all! (*calls off after Maryamma again*) Maryamma! I'm still waiting for Saint Peter! I'm a Christian!

Oh God, I bet Saint Peter won't talk to me. I'm stuck in this netherworld with this lady in a sari. (*sings briefly:*) Who's sari now? (*depressed*) Pretty good joke, huh?

I'm feeling tired. I'm afraid they're gonna send me back, like some soldier sent back to the front over and over and over. Some of them kill themselves rather than stay there . . . that's what I did. But it doesn't stop it. Oh God, suicide isn't an out anymore, it's just a doorway to another awful life!

Oh that last life. Poor little Ginny, there wasn't any hope for her. And even though she was fat, I could tell she was going to live 'til ninety or something, suffering through an endless succession of tedious days and tedious nights . . . that's a phrase from *Uncle Vanya*, or rather a translation of it, the real play's in Russian, I don't know the Russian, I saw Rex in *Uncle Vanya*, he was very good. Oh God I'm getting sleepy . . . my force of will is feeling weak . . . uh oh . . . Maryamma! Saint Peter! . . .

Whoosh sounds. Wind.

Not now, I'm busy, come back later. Go away. Maryamma! . . . Saint Peter!

Lights off of Veronica.

The sound of returning to earth continues.

SCENE 11

Lights up. We're in a grassy spot. A dog house might be nearby.

37

Veronica is standing, looking off. A MAN *in jeans and a sports shirt comes in, friendly. He is played by same actor who played Father 1 and Father 2.*

MAN   Here, boy. Come here.

At the sound of his voice, Veronica barks happily and runs up to him, thrilled to see him. She is, obviously, a dog. Perhaps a golden retriever.

It might be best if the actress played the dog standing, rather than getting on all fours. But otherwise she should do her best to seem like a dog.

VERONICA (*barks happily*)   Rrrrrrfff rrrrrrrrfff rrrrrrrrrrrfff!

MAN   That's a good boy. Go get the ball!

He throws a ball out.

Veronica runs after it, and puts the ball in her mouth. With her hand, maybe, she indicates a wagging tail—puts hand behind her back near her buttocks and moves it happily back and forth. She runs back to the Man.

In this life, the dog is really, really happy. Veronica's adult doesn't break through. Just a happy life, primarily.

Good boy! Now give me the ball. Lonnie, come on, give it to me.

The man tries to take the ball from her mouth, but she playfully resists for a while. He acts like he's going to give up and go away, and then she abruptly drops the ball. He picks the ball up again, and she then looks super-attentive, and does the hand-wagging-the-tail thing like mad. Pants, excited.

The man prepares to throw it out again.

Okay, good boy, get it now!

Man throws the ball again.

Veronica runs after it, panting happily. She gets it in her mouth and runs back to him.

Good boy. You want a treat?

Veronica is thrilled out of her mind. Wags tail, looks ecstatic. Man gives imaginary treat and Veronica indicates she's chewing it up, very happy.

Good boy. Now, go to your bed for a while, I have to go to work.

Veronica is crestfallen . . . she knows he's leaving, doesn't want him to go. BIG mood change.

VERONICA (*whimpers slightly*)   Errrrrrrrr . . . errrrrrrr. . . .

MAN   I know. But I'll be back later. I have to go to work. You be a good dog. That's right, Lonnie. Good boy.

The Man pats her on the head, then exits.

Veronica looks sad. Is very still. Just stares. Then looks around, not too interested in anything.

Then she has some sort of happy thought. It makes her wag her tail like mad, her face lights up very, very happy. It makes her pant happily too.

Then the thought passes, and she returns to silence and just staring again. She stays that way a few beats. Time passes.

Man comes back.

I'm back. I know I'm later than usual but . . .

At the sound of his returning voice Veronica is thrilled out of her mind, wags her tail again, and rushes over to him, barking happily.

VERONICA   Rrrrrrf, rrrrrrrf, rrrrrrrrf! Rrrrrrf, rrrrrrrf, rrrrrrrrf!

MAN   Good boy. You're so good. If I was late for my girlfriend, she'd just go, "Where were you? Why didn't you call?" Dogs are so good. Good boy, good boy. Wanna go for a run?

Veronica pants and jumps up and down, tail wagging.

Good boy! That's a good boy!

The Man and Veronica run off happily, to the park.

Lights dim, the grassy scene and the dog house disappear.

SCENE 12

We are suddenly back in the bardo. Maryamma is there. Veronica enters, looking happy.

VERONICA   Oh I feel refreshed after that.

MARYAMMA   Yes, your aura is a little less tweedy.

VERONICA   I can't remember much of it, actually. But it was nice.

MARYAMMA   What do you remember?

VERONICA   Ummm . . . smells. Running in the park. Being patted on the head. Good God, was I a dog?

MARYAMMA   Yes.

VERONICA   Oh. Well I liked it. I think I liked it more than any of the human incarnations. I don't remember worrying and thinking ahead. I just seemed happy in the present. I don't remember dying, how did I die?

MARYAMMA   Well, let me show you.

Maryamma and Veronica are on one part of the stage. The lighting changes on another part of the stage, and is on earth, somewhere near the park the Man and the dog went. The Man comes on happy, with energy.

MAN   Good boy! Be careful of the cars. That's a good boy.

Sound of a tire screeching, terrible car crash.

Oh no! Lonnie!!!

The man is in shock, upset.

Enter Mother 1 from the first baby scene. Dressed either the same, or very recognizable from that earlier scene. She runs in, also upset.

MOTHER 1   I'm so sorry!

MAN   You killed my dog.

MOTHER 1 It was my son actually. I was following in my car.

MAN Following him?

MOTHER 1 Well, he's only sixteen and he doesn't have his license and he was drunk and I couldn't stop him from driving . . . his father and I are terrible at discipline. It's really our fault I imagine. Would you be willing not to call the police? I'll get you another dog. I'll pay you.

MAN Pay me? Not to report this. Are you crazy?

MOTHER 1 Oh please, it will hurt his record if he's been driving drunk at sixteen without a license.

MAN It's not just my dog. He killed two people.

MOTHER 1 He did?

The Man points offstage. Mother 1 looks offstage, gasps.

Oh my God. I didn't see them. Oh dear. How much money can I give you to buy your silence? Would ten thousand dollars work?

MAN I'm sorry. I have to call the police. Your son is a menace.

MOTHER 1 It's not his fault! It's our fault. We spoiled him. He's our second child, and our first one was killed by our dog, and we felt such guilt. . . .

Veronica "gets" it now, who hit her in the car, and she doesn't care for it. Looks over at Maryamma, who tries not to give too much of a response.

MAN Killed by your dog?

MOTHER 1 Oh that's not why our son hit your dog, he likes dogs, I'm the one who has mixed feelings about them, but I'd never hit one with a car, I just would be more stringent about leaving it alone with a baby. But, you see, we spoiled him . . . and this will ruin his life if the police get called. The two people are already dead, it won't help them to punish my son.

MAN I'm going to find a phone right now.

Exits with purpose, and also to get away from her.

MOTHER 1 (*calls after him*) Oh you're a heartless person! (*calls in the direction of where the car crash was*) Run for the hills, Timmy! Mummy and Daddy will find you later. Run, darling. No, leave the vodka bottle behind, dear. We love you! Oh God. I need a drink.

Mother 1 walks or runs in the direction of Timmy, very discouraged.

The "on earth" lighting goes away, and we're back in the bardo.

Maryamma is looking at Veronica, who looks annoyed.

MARYAMMA Any comments?

VERONICA I suppose you want me to feel guilty. It's not my fault how they brought up their son. They've clearly done a bad job.

MARYAMMA I'm not interested in guilt. I'm interested if you can learn any lessons from your experiences and from their repercussions.

VERONICA You and these lessons. All right—I shouldn't have urged that dog to kill me when I was two weeks old, that was suicide which apparently is frowned upon; and what d'ya know, lo and behold, in a stunning ironic twist, when I reincarnate as a dog, I am killed by the messed-up and tragic son that I created by inviting that earlier dog to end my life in that quick and violent manner. So the lesson is . . . I'm bad, I'm bad, kick me when I'm down, I'm bad.

MARYAMMA The lesson is never: I am bad. At our core we are not bad. The lesson can be: I should not commit suicide. It could be: I must be aware my actions have an impact on other people.

VERONICA Yes, yes, fine. Well, great, I thought I had a good time as a dog, and now it turns out it was just a setup to make me feel crummy and punished.

MARYAMMA You set yourself up, that's one of the lessons.

VERONICA   If you say the word "lesson" one more time, I will have to sit on your chest and hold my hand over your mouth to prevent any more comments from you.

MARYAMMA *(laughs)*   Oh, you are a tough nut to crack, Miss Witherspoon. All right, let's forget about the drunk sixteen-year-old for now . . . and you're partially right, of course, your actions impacted the situation but they made their own choices.

VERONICA   Well thank you!

MARYAMMA   But you liked being a dog. Tell me about it.

VERONICA   It was relaxing. I was happy most of the time. I liked sniffing things in the grass. I liked running after the ball. I felt very much in the present.

MARYAMMA   Being in the present. That is a very good less . . . *(stops herself from saying "lesson")* . . . enlightenment to comprehend. Notice I didn't use the "L" word.

VERONICA   Yes. And I so appreciate it.

MARYAMMA   You're welcome.

VERONICA   What happened to Saint Peter?

MARYAMMA   I couldn't find him. But I put in a request. Rest for a while. Have some ginger tea. I'll be back later.

Maryamma exits.

VERONICA   Where do I get the ginger tea?

No answer.

Typical. Oh well. Let me rest a minute.

She sits back in her chair, tired. She closes her eyes. Then there is a VOICE—*a soothing, male voice. Very soothing. Veronica opens her eyes, listens.*

43

VOICE Welcome to the General Anesthesia Afterlife, available for Jewish people and Albert Camus and Jean-Paul Sartre. Think of nothing. Think of nothing. Nothingness. Blankness.

VERONICA Oh thank goodness.

VOICE Nothing. Nothingness. Blankness.

VERONICA Oh this is lovely. (*closes her eyes in pleasure; keeps them closed*)

VOICE Nothing. No thing. The absence of color. The absence of sound. Rest in the quiet of nothing. Negative numbers. Minus one. Minus two. Minus three. Minus one hundred thousand seven hundred and thirty-three.
Blank. Blank. Blank. Blunk. Blenk. You could be getting a colonoscopy, and you wouldn't even be aware. Blank. Blunk. Blenk. Blink. Blink of an eye, and there's nothing. Nothing. Absence of consciousness. Forgetting. No memory. No thoughts. Blankness.

Right after the Voice says "you wouldn't even be aware" in his recitation above, things start happening on the stage.

SCENE 13

Suddenly Mother 2 and Father 2 are back, the trailer trash parents of Ginny.

Mother 2 and Father 2 are in the same position they were in the first "trailer trash" scene, but the bassinet isn't there, though they look at the spot where it was as if it is still there. Even if there was much of a set for the trailer trash family, it may not all return at this time.

Veronica stays seated, seemingly asleep. Her face begins to show discomfort. As the male Voice fades away, she can register that something upsetting is impinging on her consciousness when she hears Mother 2's and Father 2's voices.

MOTHER 2   Hey, baby. Gee, it's kind of a fat baby, isn't it?

FATHER 2   Yeah, it's gonna have your fat ass.

Veronica opens her eyes, very disturbed.

MOTHER 2   Shut up. It's gonna have your greasy hair and damaged brain cells.

FATHER 2   Yeah, well I had fun damaging them.

MOTHER 2   Good for you. Why isn't the baby responding? Is it dead? Hey, fat ass! You dead?

VERONICA   Oh God. I've done this one.

From here the familiar scene of Mother 2 and Father 2 seems to skip ahead, like a record skipping, or like a DVD fast-forwarding where you see a snippet of something and then it jumps ahead to a later snippet.

Mother 2 and Father 2 should re-create their previous staging, though some variations are okay. Oftentimes they say parts of a sentence, not the whole sentence. The words themselves need not be sped up, but the transitions moving past the "missing sections" should be fast.

And there probably should be odd sounds in the background, a mechanical noise that somehow adds to the feeling that this isn't "normal" life, but is moving ahead in snippets.

FATHER 2   I shot the dog.

MOTHER 2   Is the baby defective?

FATHER 2   Well it came out your fat ass.

MOTHER 2   Hey, Ginny. Hey, Ginny!

This calling of her name makes Veronica enter the scene as a participant—though she doesn't leave her chair, she doesn't enter into their physical space. But she re-becomes little Ginny living this past life, though still seated in her bardo chair.

Wipe your mouth, look like a pig.

VERONICA   Am I pretty?

MOTHER 2   . . . pig

VERONICA   . . . hungry.

MOTHER 2   We're doin' home schoolin'.

FATHER 2   I'm overdosing. (*falls down dead*)

MOTHER 2   Oh fuck.

VERONICA   Dad? You dead?

MOTHER 2   What's seven times seven?

GINNY   Fifty-six.

MOTHER 2   (*slaps the air where Ginny would be; we hear a slap sound*)   Ow!

MOTHER 2   You're going to public school.

GINNY   Fine.

MOTHER 2   (*slaps her again*)   Ow!

   The Teacher arrives. Her desk and chair should arrive back too.

TEACHER   . . . must be Mrs. Fortunata.

MOTHER 2   Did ya punch him?

TEACHER   Virginia seems lost.

MOTHER 2   She don't listen. (*swats her on the head again, by hitting the air where she would've been*)

VERONICA   Ow!

TEACHER   . . . no hitting!

MOTHER 2   . . . socialist crap . . . hit your kids.

VERONICA   . . . you don't know nothin'.

46

MOTHER 2   respect . . . fat pig.

TEACHER   STOP IT, STOP IT!

VERONICA   . . . overdose like Daddy

MOTHER 2   too young

TEACHER   STOP IT, STOP IT!

MOTHER 2   You stop it!

TEACHER   Counseling!

MOTHER 2   Liquor store! Come on . . . ice cream!

TEACHER   Oy.

Mother 2 exits, as if she is taking Veronica/Ginny off with her. The Teacher looks exhausted.

Sounds of playground, as happened in previous scene with the Cockney drug dealer. We hear the sound of the drug dealer singing "London Bridge Is Falling Down," though it's a bit distant, a bit distorted. Veronica looks up at the sound of his song. She remembers what happened after he left her in the playground.

Veronica stands and crosses into the school space with the Teacher.

SCENE 14

Veronica has become Ginny again. The skipping ahead now stops. And background noise stops as well.

VERONICA   'Scuse me.

TEACHER   Virginia. I . . . uh. . . have been thinking of you since our meeting with your mother.

VERONICA   I got some money for my birthday, and I bought some pills. You know, happy pills. But then I didn't use them.

TEACHER (*not sure what to say*)   All right.

47

VERONICA   I saw this old, old movie about Liza Doolittle and she meets Professor Higgins, and I didn't like him, there's something that grosses me out about him, I think he's mean, and selfish and he don't really care about Liza although at the end she comes back to him but then he just wants her to hand him his slippers like she's the maid or something. But he does teach her things. And her life gets better.

TEACHER   *My Fair Lady.* You saw *My Fair Lady.*

VERONICA   Yes, and I saw her life got better, and she dressed better and she talked better. And I wondered if you could teach me. (*suddenly afraid there's no way the Teacher will say yes*) You're probably too busy. But I wondered if maybe you weren't.

TEACHER   (*looks at her closely; makes decision*)   I'd like to teach you. I'd need you to work hard. But if you worked hard, I'd work hard with you.

Veronica/Ginny is shocked she got a yes to her question. And deeply grateful. It doesn't seem possible in the world.

VERONICA   (*softly*)   Wow. Thank you.

Lights dim and come up again. Or the lights on them change substantially.

SCENE 15

The classroom. A few weeks later.

TEACHER   (*reciting as a lesson*)   In Hartford, Hereford, and Hampshire, hurricanes hardly ever happen.

VERONICA   But hurricanes are happening more now. And tornados. And meteorites.

TEACHER   Yes, I guess that's true. The weather has been changing. (*teaching again*) The rain in Spain stays mainly in the plain.

VERONICA   Will that be on the SATs?

TEACHER Well this is about speaking.

VERONICA Oh. The rine in Spine sties minely on the pline.

TEACHER No, Ginny. Plain.

VERONICA I know, I'm pretending to be Cockney.

TEACHER Oh. (*laughs; hadn't gotten it; now recites again, with energy*) Sister Susie's sewing shirts for soldiers. Such skill at sewing shirts my shy young sister Susie shows. Some soldiers write epistles, say they'd sooner sleep on thistles than the soft and saucy shirts for soldiers sister Susie sews.

VERONICA What?

TEACHER (*as if this is teaching too, but her voice starts to fade as it goes on, and she begins to exit, still speaking*) Negative numbers. Minus one. Minus two. Minus three. Minus four. Minus one hundred thousand seven hundred and thirty-three. Minus one hundred thousand seven hundred and thirty-four.

Maybe the soothing Man's voice joins the Teacher's voice as she's exiting. Or not. In any case, the lights dim down and the Teacher exits.

Veronica leaves the school area, and goes to a different area, defined tightly by light.

SCENE 16

Mother 2 comes into the space, very much the worse for wear. She looks like she's gone back to using drugs, her hair is messy, and she's a little nondistinct, like a drunk who makes her points emphatically but messily.

From their behavior together, we assume they are in their house or trailer. Veronica/Ginny is either practicing something from a book she's holding—moving her mouth, trying to memorize it for an assignment— or she's just doing stretching exercises, trying to ignore her mother.

As the scene goes on, we realize Veronica/Ginny is two to three years older. She's a bit more sure of herself.

MOTHER 2 I don't want you seeing that teacher anymore. She's filling your head with lies. You're gonna fail, and I don't want you to forget it.

VERONICA Why don't you take an overdose and die?

MOTHER 2 The Bible says, "Honor your parents." Did I kill you? Did I abort you? Did I pour scalding water on your private parts? Well, did I?

VERONICA No.

MOTHER 2 And can you say thank you?

VERONICA Thank you for not pouring scalding water on my private parts.

A large metal thing suddenly falls from the sky—as happened in the beginning of the play. Both Veronica and Mother 2 scream.

MOTHER 2 AND VERONICA Aaaaaaaaaaaaghhh!!!

MOTHER 2 Damn it! The sky is falling, the sky is falling!

VERONICA It's one of those meteorites.

MOTHER 2 It's not a piece of plane or something?

VERONICA No.

MOTHER 2 Remember when the toilet from that plane dropped down and killed the postman?

VERONICA Well, it doesn't look like a toilet, does it?

Sound of terrible wind.

MOTHER 2 Uh-oh. Another torpedo.

VERONICA Tornado, not torpedo.

MOTHER 2 Don't talk back.

VERONICA Didn't we have a hurricane yesterday? What's the matter with the weather?

MOTHER 2 I don't know, something about the air. Go to the cellar.

VERONICA We don't have a cellar.

MOTHER 2 Well get away from the window then.

Terrible wind. We hear the sudden sound of a window breaking. Lights go out totally briefly. Maybe Mother 2 screams. Lots of noise. It sounds like a scary storm.

Wind stops. Quiet. Lights come back up.

SCENE 17

Lights focus back on the school area. There is a banner: "Congratulations, Graduates." We see Veronica standing, waiting to speak. The Teacher is also onstage, wearing a corsage, standing off to the side and watching Veronica proudly. Mother 2 is not there.

VERONICA I am so proud to be graduating today. I never thought I would be chosen as the commencement speaker. In Hartford, Hereford, and Hampshire, hurricanes hardly ever happen. That's from a movie with Rex Harrison back many years ago.

Lights go out or, for theater purposes, they greatly dim.

Oh dear. It's hard to give a commencement speech in the dark. But of course the weather is so changeable from minute to minute the lights are always going out. But then you know that. You're sitting in the dark as well. But we can get used to so many things.

The lights suddenly come up to normal, bright levels, as if electricity has been restored. There's a little buzz when it comes back on.

Oh, that's good. Now I can see you. I am so grateful to my teacher Mrs. Donaldson. She is the mother I never had.

Mother 2, still looking a wreck, briefly juts her head in from the side of the stage.

MOTHER 2 (*shouts in Ginny's direction*)   I am your mother! (*promptly disappears off again*)

VERONICA (*shouting after her in full, expressed fury*)   SHUT UP, YOU DRUG-ADDICTED, SADISTIC SUBHUMAN PIECE OF SHIT! (*shocked at herself, and abashed; to audience:*) I'm so sorry! That's not part of my commencement address. (*looks back at the Teacher, who indicates not to worry, just go on*) We're living in a scary world. Volatile, turbulent. Small chunks of meteorites keep braining us on the head. Sometimes we have tornados five days in a row. Then there will be a massive snowstorm in July. Drought in some states, while others receive seven inches of rain in two hours and become flooded. The government says they must do further study before anything can be done.

The sound of a rumble begins.

Uh oh. Another earthquake. Hold on to your seats and hope the ceiling doesn't fall.

Lights go dim again.

There they go again.

Sound of earthquake noises. Alarming. Veronica tries to speak over it.

Everyone remain calm. It's probably just a small one. Say your mantras. Blankness. The absence of color. The absence of sound. Negative numbers. Minus one. Minus two. Minus three. Minus one hundred thousand seven hundred and thirty-three. Blank. Blank. Blink of an eye, and then nothing. Forgetting. No memory. No thoughts. Blankness.

The lights fade to black during the above. The Teacher exits. Veronica, while saying the mantra words, starts making her way to her chair in the bardo. The sounds crescendo as the lights go to black.

The terrible sounds stop. Lights come up. Back in the bardo.

Veronica is seated on her chair. Her eyes are closed. She opens them. Maryamma is standing over her.

MARYAMMA   Miss Witherspoon, you've been asleep for several decades. How are you feeling?

VERONICA   Decades? Good Lord. Well I feel very rested. Though I also feel sort of stirred up.

MARYAMMA   I relented. I decided your spirit needed to replenish itself, and so we let you have the afterlife you had requested.

VERONICA   You mean the anesthesia afterlife. But I'm confused. I seemed to have relived another life. It was better, and I was the commencement speaker. . . . I took your advice, and I asked the teacher for help. But was it part of the anesthesia afterlife or was I living an alternative reality?

MARYAMMA   Exactly.

VERONICA   But that was an either-or question. What do you mean "exactly"?

MARYAMMA   Miss Witherspoon, your aura is looking a little lighter, can you feel it?

VERONICA   I think I can a little. Something was wrong with the weather. Is that reality or was that part of a dream?

MARYAMMA   Exactly. More government study. Always a sign of lies and obfuscation.

VERONICA   Next time, can I have the anesthesia afterlife but no alternative realities? Just a nice rest, you know.

MARYAMMA   I have a treat for you. Someone has asked to speak with you.

VERONICA   Oh?

MARYAMMA   Yes. Look who's here.

Enter a BLACK WOMAN *in a flowered dress and a going-to-church hat. She seems friendly.*

BLACK WOMAN   Hello.

VERONICA   Hello.

BLACK WOMAN   Hello.

VERONICA (*uncertain*)   Hello. Mrs. Donaldson?

BLACK WOMAN   I'm Jesus Christ. I wanted to meet you before you reincarnate for your next life.

VERONICA (*a bit taken aback; smiles, wonders if she's being kidded*) You look like the teacher I was just dreaming about.

BLACK WOMAN   Ah, so my appearance to you was foretold in a dream?

VERONICA   Not exactly. Someone who looked like you, but without the hat. She was a teacher. And historically Jesus Christ was a man, was he not?

BLACK WOMAN   I take many forms. Today I'm a black woman. Do you like my hat?

VERONICA   It's okay.

BLACK WOMAN   Really? I think it's nicer than okay, but no matter. I told Maryamma I wanted to speak to you because in your next life I want you to point out to people all the ways that they are not following me.

VERONICA   Well I was telling Maryamma I'm hoping for more of the anesthesia afterlife.

BLACK WOMAN   I've made a list for you of things I've said that people are ignoring. Number one: Blessed are the meek for they shall inherit the earth. Number two: Blessed are the merciful for they shall receive mercy.

VERONICA Oh yes, the Beatitudes. They're lovely.

BLACK WOMAN Thank you. Though I mean for them to be lived, not just admired as lovely.

VERONICA Well I'm sure everyone understands that.

BLACK WOMAN Really? Number three: Let him who is without sin cast the first stone. Likewise, judge not lest ye be judged.

VERONICA Ah yes. Well it's hard not to judge, isn't it, it sort of happens automatically I think.

BLACK WOMAN The path I ask of people is hard. Number four: Love God, and love thy neighbor as thyself.

VERONICA You know, I'm not really a Christian anymore. I don't know what I am.

BLACK WOMAN Number five: It is easier for a camel to pass through the eye of a needle than for a rich man to get into heaven.

VERONICA I see. Is there an income cutoff where that comes into effect?

BLACK WOMAN No there's no cutoff. Look at the lilies of the field, and then just have a little bit more than they do, and that'll be fine.

VERONICA I see.

BLACK WOMAN Number six: If thy eye offend thee, pluck it out.

VERONICA Pluck it out?

BLACK WOMAN No, that's a hard one. Forget that one. Number seven: What does it profit a man if he gain the whole world, and loses his soul?

VERONICA Yes, that's a good one.

BLACK WOMAN (*with friendly encouragement*) I really need you to get down there and shake these people up!

VERONICA (*laughs weakly*)   Oh well, I'm not really much of a messenger. Why don't you go back there and say these things?

BLACK WOMAN   I did that once, now it's somebody else's turn! I look down at people on earth not following what I said, and I just get riled up. (*starting to get worked up*) I mean, I said, "Blessed are the merciful," right, that's clear, right? I didn't say, Blessed are those who proclaim themselves holier than others and read the Book of Revelation as if it's an instruction booklet, and sit around waiting for the Rapture, when they think I'm going to bring all these holy folk up to heaven, and we're gonna sit up there together and watch Jews and atheists and non-Christians writhe about in agony for years and years. And we'll watch that as what?—entertainment? Enjoyable revenge?

VERONICA   The Book of Revelation is a particularly dense book, isn't it? I could never make sense of it.

BLACK WOMAN   That's a pleasingly humble reaction. You see, I'm concerned with the misuse of my name. Answer me a question. Didn't I say, "Blessed are the peacemakers"? That's number eight. Blessed are the peacemakers.

VERONICA   Please stop reciting these numbers to me, I'm actually mostly in agreement.

BLACK WOMAN   If you're in agreement, why won't you help?

VERONICA   Well . . . I don't know, I just don't want to. Besides people have gotten very comfortable with their own interpretations of Christianity. It would be very hard to budge them, especially if I had to say, "Oh, and by the way, I was told this by some 'black woman in a hat' who said she was Jesus Christ."

BLACK WOMAN   I'll be a black woman on Tuesday if I want, and a Pakistani man on Wednesday, and a ham sandwich on Thursday. I'm communicating in parable, plus I also have a sense of humor. (*harshly*) Do you like my hat?

VERONICA   It's not my place to fix the world. If you want to fix it, you go down there again and fix it yourself. And you should go as a floating ham sandwich; I bet people will really pay attention to you then. But leave me out of it. I have not liked the world, and it has not liked me, and I thought once you died, it was over, and that's what I am, I'm over. Over and out. Got it?

BLACK WOMAN   Got it. (*to Maryamma*) I thought you said she would be receptive.

MARYAMMA   Oh, give her time.

VERONICA   Give me a lot of time. Eternity, preferably.

MARYAMMA   Oh look who's coming now.

Enter GANDALF. *Dressed like Ian McKellen in the* Lord of the Rings *movies. Gray beard, long white robe, staff. Charismatic, full of wisdom. He has a British accent and a rich, sonorous sound to his speaking voice.*

Miss Witherspoon, this is Gandalf. He asked to speak with you as well.

GANDALF   Hello, Miss Witherspoon.

VERONICA   Hello. (*polite*) And have you met Jesus?

GANDALF (*to Black Woman*)   Oh yes, of course. Sorry I didn't recognize you. I thought you were Josephine Baker.

BLACK WOMAN   Thank you. I thought you were Rex Harrison.

VERONICA   What?

GANDALF   Well I do have a British accent.

BLACK WOMAN   I should warn you, she's difficult.

GANDALF (*wishing to be the charming diplomat*)   Well, I'm sure she's not difficult, perhaps just . . . perplexed.

BLACK WOMAN   Oh she's perplexed all right.

GANDALF (*addressing Veronica*)   Miss Witherspoon, Jesus Christ and I, and Mr. Gandhi, who's not able to be here today, have all been meeting with the souls in the bardo, urging them to move through their spiritual evolution faster than they've been doing, because middle earth is in danger of extinction, and looking at it from the netherworld, it all seems so unnecessary and pointless and savage. And so we need the souls who are in process to be engaged, they cannot go live through eighty and ninety years and only learn tiny, tiny lessons. We need things to move faster.

VERONICA (*to Black Woman*/JESUS)   What did you say about Rex Harrison?

GANDALF   Miss Witherspoon, your disagreements with Mr. Harrison are taking up far too much of your mental energy. Let it go. Let it go.

VERONICA   Yes, but. . .

GANDALF   No, let it go. Try it, it's easier than you think. Stop your argument with Mr. Harrison. Just stop. Let it go.

VERONICA (*thinks*)   Okay. (*really thinks about letting it go; thinks some more; lets go*) Okay. (*bit surprised; feels lighter*)

GANDALF   Now you see we started out life brutally, with no language, no skills, the caveman days, and we focused only on survival. And that went on for several centuries. Then we saw the need for other people, and that strength can come from bonding together, and so then we became tribal. Our group becomes our tribe. Our tribe is the important one, and if there are other tribes, who might want the things we want for our survival, those other tribes become our enemy. And so warfare begins, and tribes become nations, and there are more and more terrible weapons, and scientists invent more and more horrible ways in which to kill people, and the spiritual evolution is taking too long. There must be a quantum leap. People must move forward faster.

BLACK WOMAN   Number nine.

VERONICA   Stop. I'm not a leader. Why are you pushing me about this?

GANDALF   You have more strength than you know, Miss Witherspoon.

BLACK WOMAN   You do. You're using your strength to resist. Use it for something else. Be brave. Not like when you knew your sister wasn't a witch and you didn't speak up for her in the Salem witch trials.

VERONICA   I didn't want to be killed too, is that so terrible?

BLACK WOMAN   You're saying that to someone who was crucified?

MARYAMMA   I thought you didn't remember your life in Salem.

VERONICA   Well I didn't. But now I do. Are you happy?

MARYAMMA   I'm always happy. (*pause*) Let's everybody find a place of calm, everybody's aura is getting a little cloudy.

Maryamma uses her hands to brush away the air around her head and upper body; what she does looks elegant and easy.

Gandalf and Black Woman do somewhat similar things, but Gandalf's motions are a bit more minimalist, and Black Woman has a larger, somewhat forceful way with aura cleansing.

But bottom line, they wave their hands around their head and upper body, in order to "cleanse their auras."

Veronica watches this, and then gives it a shot, and does the same thing, but with a certain "I don't believe in this" look on her face.

They all finish their cleansing of auras.

Would anyone like some tea?

GANDALF   Yes, I would.

BLACK WOMAN   Do you have Red Zinger?

Suddenly there is the sound of terrible turbulence.

All four people start to shake uncontrollably, as if the whole bardo was shaking like a plane during turbulence. They find it hard to stand in one place.

MARYAMMA Oh, hold on.

VERONICA What's going on?

GANDALF Just some turbulence. Hold on.

VERONICA Turbulence? In the bardo?

GANDALF Yes. I was hoping this wouldn't happen.

VERONICA What wouldn't happen?

BLACK WOMAN We were afraid of this. India and Pakistan have exchanged nuclear attacks, and North Korea has bombed South Korea. And terrorists have set off biological attacks in London, Madrid, Rome, and New York. And the United States has bombed Iraq, Syria, and Iran. And so we're feeling turbulence up here. But don't worry. It will pass, and then we can get back to discussing your next incarnation.

The turbulence and shaking continues for a bit. Then it stops.

Oh thank goodness. It's over, for now at least.

MARYAMMA Perhaps that tea now.

VERONICA Wait. "Discuss my next incarnation." I don't want to go back there, especially after what you told me just happened. What does the world look like?

GANDALF Well not good. It's funny, all that worry about Russia and the United States and their nuclear standoff, and then this is how the nuclear nightmare unfolds with all these smaller states, and even individuals, opening Pandora's box below.

VERONICA I was always afraid of that myth, Pandora's box.

GANDALF With good cause. So in your next reincarnation, Miss Witherspoon, you must work for global understanding . . . the various tribes must move past their tribal mentalities, and find a way to embrace their interdependence.

BLACK WOMAN   That's right! Move past it!

VERONICA   Well easier said than done, no?

GANDALF   Your next life I think you'll be in the Middle East. You will all be dying of radiation poisoning, and you must convince people of the need for nonviolence.

VERONICA   I am not Mahatma Gandhi. I am an emotionally damaged woman with poor follow-through and little bravery. And I am not about to be sent back to live in a new Stone Age. I simply refuse.

MARYAMMA   Miss Witherspoon, it is not your soul's right to refuse.

VERONICA   (*realizes she must come up with an alternate plan*)   Look, I see I wasted those other lives I had. Let me go back there, before these things have happened, and relive one of those lives. And I'll try to do some of what you say.

BLACK WOMAN   "Try" is a bad word. Don't "try" to do it. Do it.

MARYAMMA   Yes, but you can't go back and live a life you've already lived. That's not how it works.

VERONICA   Well, didn't I just relive Ginny's life? Or part of it? And her life got better. Maybe it was a dream, but maybe it wasn't. And what about quantum physics and the speed of light . . . and . . . and . . . "there are more things in heaven and earth, Horatio, than are dreamt of in your . . . puny little brain." Who says time has to go forward?—maybe it can go backwards. And didn't one of you say, "Faith can move mountains"?

BLACK WOMAN   I think that was Norman Vincent Peale.

VERONICA   Well he's not the only one who's said it. Others have too. So I say anything is possible too. I've stopped my reincarnation several times, which this woman says I shouldn't have been able to do, I say I can reincarnate BACK in time when there's still hope. I don't want to live in what you say you're sending me to.

MARYAMMA (*regretfully*)   The bardo has certain rules. . . .

GANDALF   No. Miss Witherspoon is right. If her soul can reincarnate backwards in time, and relive a life better and make the outcome of the world better . . . we should let her.

MARYAMMA   Well "let her," sure. But is it actually doable?

BLACK WOMAN   Maybe I should redo the crucifixion. No that's too complicated. Never mind.

VERONICA   Yes, I'll go back. I just can't go forward, let me try to clear up the mess in the past . . . (*senses Black Woman's disapproval*) . . . sorry, I won't use the word "try," let me CLEAR up the mess in the past, and I don't know, I guess from the sound of it, I'm meant to be a pacifist Christian who teaches the importance of breaking down tribal differences.

BLACK WOMAN   And I'm just one of the faces of God, include that.

VERONICA   Okay.

GANDALF   Miss Witherspoon, stand in the place from which you shall return to a previous time.

Veronica goes back to her chair, which is the "usual" spot where the returns to earth have taken place. She stands by the chair, doesn't sit.

Black Woman, Gandalf, and Maryamma all start to exit, but with their eyes on Veronica as they leave.

BLACK WOMAN   Good luck!

GANDALF   You will not be alone. Other souls will follow you back as well.

BLACK WOMAN   In Hartford, Hereford, and Hampshire, hurricanes hardly happen. Ask for help.

MARYAMMA   Goodbye, Miss Witherspoon, I'll have that ginger tea ready when you return.

Veronica is alone onstage now. The "returning to earth" whoosh sounds begin. Veronica's face doesn't struggle, she's resigned and almost willing to go back now.

The sounds of "returning to earth"—wind, music, etc.—continue in intensity. As Veronica is about to "whoosh" down to earth, the lights dim to black, and the sounds intensify.

SCENE 19

Lights come back up. We are back in the nursery room of the first baby scene, with the first Mother.

The Mother is found in light, dressed as she was in the first scene, and looking down at the bassinet.

Veronica is in the bassinet, in the same bonnet. She's looking out initially, not quite sure where's she going to find herself.

MOTHER   Hello, darling. Hello there. Yes. It's Mommy. Hello. Good morning. How did precious sleep?

VERONICA (*her adult self speaking*)   Oh God, did it work? I hope I'm not in Iraq or Syria or something. Where am I? (*looks around*)

MOTHER   Hello, darling. Welcome to your home in Connecticut.

VERONICA   Connecticut, thank God! I think this is back in time. I'm pretty sure. (*speaks as baby*) Ga ga. Goo goo. Ma-ma-ma! Ma-ma-ma!

MOTHER   One less syllable, dear. Ma-ma. Ma-ma.

VERONICA   Ma-ma-ma. Ma-ma-ma. (*adult self*) Oh, God I've got to relearn language. Oh Lord it takes too long. I better be a prodigy, that's all I can say.

MOTHER   What, dear?

VERONICA   Google, google.

MOTHER   Yes, Google that's a search engine. Oh, David, she's very chatty this morning. She almost said "Mama."

Enter David, the Father. He is in a suit, dressed for work.

He, though, also has Gandalf's hair and long beard. And is played by same actor who played Gandalf. His manner of speaking, though, is how he spoke as the original father.

FATHER   Talkative, is she? Good morning, sweet pea.

MOTHER   Good God, David! When did you grow that beard? And the hair?

Veronica notices his hair and beard too. And recognizes him as Gandalf.

FATHER   Oh, over the last few weeks.

MOTHER   Well how could I have not noticed it?

FATHER   You've been focused on Miss Witherspoon.

MOTHER   Who?

FATHER   You know, the old nursery rhyme. Whither the spoon goes, whither the fork. Wither-spoon.

MOTHER   I hope you're going to shave. You look like something out of *The Lord of the Rings*.

FATHER   We'll see. What a beautiful baby.

Sound of dog barking, then growling. Seemingly the dog comes into the room.

MOTHER   Oh, David, don't let Fido in here. I think he's jealous of the baby.

FATHER   He's just not used to her yet. He'll learn to accept her.

MOTHER   Well he doesn't usually show his teeth.

FATHER   He'll get used to her, if we just let them spend time together.

VERONICA (*firmly, commanding, she who must be obeyed*)   GET THE DAMN DOG OUTTA HERE!

Mother and Father look very startled.

MOTHER   David? Did she say words?

FATHER   I don't think so. She sounded very firm though.

MOTHER   I feel like she told us to get the dog out of here.

FATHER   Well maybe she's right. Let's keep the dog out of this room. Come on, Fido.

Father takes dog out.

VERONICA (*adult self, to herself*)   Okay, I need to learn language now. (*baby; speaks clearly though*) A, E, I, O, U. Aaaaaaa. Eeeeeeeee. I-iiiiiii. O-ooooooo.

Father comes backs in.

MOTHER   David, she just said the vowels.

FATHER   Babies make lots of vowel sounds.

MOTHER   No, in an organized way. She said A, E, I, O, U.

VERONICA   A, E, I, O, U.

FATHER   By George, she's got it! By George, she's got it!

VERONICA (*adult self*)   Oh God, it's Rex Harrison again. (*whispers to Father/Gandalf*) You better be nicer this time.

FATHER   Very well, I will.

MOTHER   What?

FATHER   Nothing. Well, this is clearly a prodigy baby. I can tell it's going to learn language very soon. Whither the spoon, whither the fork, the baby's a gift, brought here by the stork.

MOTHER I've never heard that rhyme.

VERONICA Ga ga. Ma-ma-ma. Google, google. Gee gee gee gee gee. Global. Global. Glo-bal.

MOTHER She keeps making words. I'm a little confused.

FATHER Well she's going to be smart, that's all.

MOTHER Oh, a smart baby. I might just prefer a happy baby.

FATHER Well there may be more need for a smart baby. Come on, let's hear the vowels again. A, E, I, O, U.

VERONICA (*very fast*) A, E, I, O, U. In Hartford, Hereford, and Hampshire.

FATHER Hurricanes hardly happen.

VERONICA Ga ga ga. Google. Alternative forms of energy. Consensus. Mediation. Diplomacy. Ga ga. Blblblblblbblblblll.

Maryamma enters, carrying a tray with tea on it.

MARYAMMA I thought you might like some tea.

Veronica does recognize Maryamma, just as she recognized the "Gandalf-ness" of the Father moments ago.

MOTHER Oh thank you, Raini. David, I don't think you've met Raini. I hired her yesterday.

FATHER Yes, while I was growing my beard. How do you do?

MARYAMMA Do you like ginger tea?

FATHER Yes, thank you.

MARYAMMA (*looks at Veronica*) What a pretty baby.

FATHER She's very smart.

MOTHER Well all parents think their baby is smart.

VERONICA   In order to survive, we must find a way to break through the centuries of stressing tribal differences, and evolve to finding tribal and human similarities.

All are startled.

MARYAMMA   She speaks in complete sentences already.

MOTHER   I know. It's unusual.

FATHER   Well, she's anxious to make a mark in the world.

MARYAMMA   What a lovely clear aura she has.

Maryamma, Father, and Mother stare down at the baby.

Veronica looks up at them. Then she looks outward.

The lights dim, but a special light stays on Veronica's face longer than on the others. Her face is the last thing we see before the lights dim to black. Her expression is a little hard to read, but it contains hope and worry. Or maybe worry and hope.

End of play.

The Beadle	Jeff Howell
The Beadle's Wife	Sheila McKenna
Edvar	Matthew Gaydos
Hedvig	Elena Passarello
Bartender 1	Larry John Meyers
Bartender 2	Jeff Howell
Clarence (*the angel*)	Larry John Meyers
George Bailey	Matthew Gaydos
Zuzu Bailey	Lauren Rose Gigliotti or Allison Hannon
Monica (*the angel*)	Elena Passarello
The Nice Mrs. Cratchit	Elena Passarello
Serena the maid	Matthew Gaydos

CHARACTERS (*in order of appearance*)

Young Jacob Marley (*child*)
Young Ebenezer Scrooge (*child*)
The Ghost
Ebenezer Scrooge
Bob Cratchit
Tiny Tim
Mrs. Bob Cratchit
Child 1 (*Cratchit Child*)
Child 2 (*Cratchit Child*)
Gentleman 1
Gentleman 2
Jacob Marley
Mr. Fezziwig
Mrs. Fezziwig
The Beadle
The Beadle's Wife
Edvar
Hedvig
Little Nell
Bartender
George
Zuzu
Clarence
The Nice Mrs. Cratchit
Lovely Irish Voice (*woman*)
Tess's Voice
Serena, a maid

ACT I

Christmastime. Dickens look, 1840s. A street in London. Two
YOUNG BOYS, *dressed in coats, hats, and scarfs, stand next to*
each other. One boy is singing.

BOY 1 (*singing sweetly*)
Hark the Herald Angels sing
Glory to the new born king

BOY 2 (*irritated, negative*)   Bah, humbug! Bah, humbug!

BOY 1 (*singing*)
Peace on earth, and mercy mild

BOY 2   Phooey! Christmas stinks! Kaplooey!

BOY 1 (*singing*)
God and sinner reconciled

BOY 2   Bah humbug! Get me a good hamburger!

BOY 1 (*continues with the song softly*)

Enter the GHOST—*a striking, theatrical black woman. She addresses*
the audience.

GHOST   Even as a child, young Ebenezer displayed a
pronounced antipathy toward Christmas. (*to Boy 2*) Merry
Christmas, Ebenezer.

YOUNG EBENEZER   Bah humbug! Give me some Christmas
pudding. I want to put bugs in your hair! Bah humbug!

GHOST   In later centuries, we would probably identify Ebenezer's
repeated saying of "Bah humbug" as a kind of seasonal Tourette's
syndrome. However, in 1843, when our story is set, we hadn't a
clue what it meant—except he was a nasty little child.

YOUNG EBENEZER Bah humbug! I hate Christmas!

GHOST (*to audience*) Hello. I am the Ghost of Christmas Past, Present, and Yet To Come, including all media yet to be invented. If you get me on DVD you can click on Special Features, and see twenty-seven other hairdo choices I have. But we're in a live theater presently, so you'll just have to accept my hair as it is.

YOUNG EBENEZER I want to put bugs in your hair!

GHOST Children are so difficult, aren't they? You should see them backstage. I'm so glad I'm a ghost and I don't have any children.

BOY 1 I like Christmas carols, but my friend Ebenezer is slowly convincing me to hate Christmas.

GHOST (*points to Boy 1*) This is young Jacob Marley. And he and Ebenezer will grow up to run a business together.

YOUNG EBENEZER I want to be very wealthy.

YOUNG JACOB Me too!

GHOST Oh you kids. I'd like to take a strap to you. But all you politically correct types don't like that. A good spanking never hurt a child, unless it got out of control and killed him, in which case it did. But I don't want to kill these children, I just want to make them behave. (*screams at the children*) BEHAVE!!! AND HAVE A BETTER ATTITUDE ABOUT CHRISTMAS!

YOUNG EBENEZER I hate Christmas. Bah, humbug.

GHOST You have Tourette's syndrome. You need to learn to be seen and not heard. (*to audience*) And now meet Ebenezer Scrooge, grown up.

Enter old EBENEZER SCROOGE. *He is sour, grumpy, cranky.*

Hello there, Mr. Scrooge. Merry Christmas to you.

EBENEZER SCROOGE Bah humbug! I'd like to put bugs in your hair!

GHOST Really, how strange. What kind of bugs?

EBENEZER SCROOGE Oh awful crawling kinds. Beetles. Spiders.

GHOST Uh-huh. Mr. Scrooge, I'd like you to meet your inner child.

EBENEZER SCROOGE What?

GHOST (*to Young Ebenezer*) Say hello to your grown-up self, Ebenezer.

YOUNG EBENEZER I hate you! (*kicks him*)

EBENEZER SCROOGE And I hate you, you little creep!

Ebenezer and Young Ebenezer struggle with each other. Young Jacob looks on, passively.

GHOST (*to audience*) What unpleasant people. I wonder if I'll be able to make them appreciate the true meaning of Christmas before the end of the evening. What do you think? How many of you don't care? Never mind, I don't want to know. I have a job to do, and I've got to do it. Okay, you two, break it up.

EBENEZER SCROOGE You should be sent to the workhouse!

YOUNG EBENEZER You should be sent to a nursing home!

GHOST Isn't it sad? Isn't it poignant and ironic how much Mr. Scrooge's younger and older selves hate each other? (*to Young Ebenezer and Ebenezer*) You're dealing with self-hatred, you two, and you don't even know it!

YOUNG JACOB Why don't I have any lines?

GHOST Why does the sun come up in the morning?

YOUNG JACOB I don't know.

GHOST Well, that's why you don't have any lines. Okay, enough of this scene. Let's move on to the next one. Ready, Mr. Scrooge?

EBENEZER SCROOGE Shut up, I don't know you. I don't think there even are Negro people in 1840s London.

GHOST I stand outside of time.

EBENEZER SCROOGE Well good for you. I haven't time for this, I'm on my way to work.

GHOST Merry Christmas.

EBENEZER SCROOGE Bah! Humbug!

YOUNG EBENEZER Bah! Humbug!

Scrooge exits, followed by Young Ebenezer and Young Jacob.

GHOST Luckily, you know, most people aren't like Mr. Scrooge here. They love Christmas as I do, and as I hope you do too.

Music begins. The Ghost looks around the stage in pleasant wonderment.

GHOST (*sings*)
London is a-buzz
London is a-glow
People mill about in groups
They wander to and fro

LONDON TOWNSPEOPLE *start to come in and gather. They mill about in groups; they wander. They point at things in the set. A wandering person may be selling toys. The children point at them. They're all very happy and interested in Christmas.*

They come onstage
From left and right
From upstage, downstage too

They come to town
They point at things
They've got a lot to do

LONDON TOWNSPEOPLE (*sing*)
We're all so excited
We're happy and delighted
The fun has been ignited
We grin from ear to ear

GHOST (*sings*)
And why is that
The reason is quite clear
That Christmas
Lovely Christmastime is near

It's nearly Christmas
Look at all the shops
The pigs are eating slops

It's nearly Christmas
The air is crisp and cold
Children good as gold

It sort of weighs a ton
This festive Christmas fun
And yet we wouldn't have it any other way!

GHOST AND LONDON TOWNSPEOPLE (*sing*)
We love Christmas
We love Christmas, Christmas day

> The CRATCHIT *family, who have been part of the above, have now milled about into a center place so they may be featured.*

> *It's* BOB CRATCHIT, *helping* TINY TIM *on his crutch. And* MRS. BOB CRATCHIT *is being warm and motherly to two of her other children,* CHILD 1 (*girl*) *and* CHILD 2 (*boy*).

GHOST (*sings*)
Here are the Cratchits
Bob and Tiny Tim
It's sweet and it's touching

Bob watches over him
This is only a glimpse
Sad to say, the child limps
It's not quite clear if there's a cure
Still Tiny Tim, his heart is pure

TINY TIM (*spoken*)   Anything sad or bad I just ignore. I love Christmas.

BOB CRATCHIT   I know you do, Tiny Tim. And your mother and I love it too. Don't we, dear?

MRS. BOB CRATCHIT (*not realizing she was going to be asked to speak*) Oh yes. What? We love Christmas very much. (*slightly weak smile, she's a bit tired*)

GHOST, THE CRATCHITS, AND LONDON TOWNSPEOPLE (*sing*)
It's nearly Christmas
Such a joyful noise
Children play with toys

It's nearly Christmas
Snow is in the air
A partridge and a pear

It melts the hearts of cranks
They learn they must give thanks
It's a time to laugh and sing and dance and play
We love Christmas, we love Christmas, Christmas day

> *Mr. Scrooge comes back onstage, still needing to get to work. He didn't mean to come back this route and is horrified to see everyone.*

A CHILD   Look—it's Mr. Scrooge!

THE CRATCHITS AND LONDON TOWNSPEOPLE (*spoken*)   MERRY CHRISTMAS, MR. SCROOGE!

> *Mr. Scrooge is horrified, and it makes him nauseous. He starts to need to vomit, covers his mouth with his hand, runs offstage.*

(*disappointed in his response*) Ahhhhhhhhhhh.

TINY TIM   Mr. Scrooge doesn't know how to celebrate Christmas, does he, Father?

BOB CRATCHIT (*laughs*)   Indeed he does not, Tiny Tim!

Everyone smiles delighted. Mrs. Bob Cratchit smiles also, but it seems a little strained.

TINY TIM   God bless us, everyone!

Everyone looks even more delighted. Mrs. Bob Cratchit looks at him, slightly sick of him, but it's subtle. It's possible we might not notice. She's trying to be agreeable and to love Christmas, mostly. It's just that, like her clothes, her nerves are threadbare.

GHOST   And God bless you, Tiny Tim!

Tiny Tim beams. In the following, done in a very musical comedy/ Oliver kind of way, Mrs. Bob Cratchit gamely moves with everyone else, but is a bit out of synch sometimes. She does not sing along with them.

EVERYONE (*except for Mrs. Bob Cratchit*) (*sings*)
It's nearly Christmas
The reindeer and the sleigh
Let nothing you dismay
It's nearly Christmas
The jingle bells ding ding
Let's go a-caroling

It's time-consuming, true

MRS. BOB CRATCHIT (*spoken, to audience*)   Yes, it is.

EVERYONE (*except for Mrs. Bob Cratchit*) (*sings*)
It makes some people blue

MRS. BOB CRATCHIT (*spoken, to audience*)   Well, a little.

EVERYONE (*except for Mrs. Bob Cratchit*) (*sings*)
And yet we wouldn't have it any other way!

MRS. BOB CRATCHIT (*spoken, to audience, laughs*)   Well I would!

EVERYONE (*except for Mrs. Bob Cratchit*) (*sings*)
We love Christmas

MRS. BOB CRATCHIT (*spoken, suddenly uncertain*)   Did I turn the
oven off?

EVERYONE (*except for Mrs. Bob Cratchit*) (*sings*)
We love Christmas

MRS. BOB CRATCHIT (*spoken, looking around worried*)   Ohhhh!
Where are the children???

EVERYONE (*except for Mrs. Bob Cratchit*) (*sings*)
We love Christmas

   Mrs. Bob Cratchit decides to join in on the final words of the song.

EVERYONE (*sings*)
Christmas day!

   *Townspeople all disperse, waving at one another or maybe the audience.
   Mrs. Bob Cratchit fiddles with Bob Cratchit's long scarf, making sure
   he's warm. Then she leads Tiny Tim and the other two children off, while
   Bob goes off in the same direction Scrooge had exited. Set change starts.*

GHOST   Well I hope you enjoyed that. Sometimes I prefer to
sing a Billie Holiday song, but "'Tain't Nobody's Business If I
Do" doesn't seem very Christmas-y. So it's time to begin our
journey of redeeming Mr. Ebenezer Scrooge. And the first place
we should go is his place of work, the office of Scrooge and
Marley. Because Mr. Scrooge felt sick to his stomach, luckily
Bob Cratchit was able to get there first. (*seeing the set is complete:*)
Ah, and here's the set change.

SCENE 2

   Scrooge's office.

   *Bob Cratchit, a mild-mannered, suffering blob of a man, sits at his
   desk, shivering, and writing in a notebook.*

Nearby, set off somewhat, is Scrooge's desk. Near his desk TWO GENTLEMEN *in top coats are standing, waiting for him.*

Scrooge enters in a bad mood.

BOB CRATCHIT   Good morning, Mr. Scrooge.

EBENEZER SCROOGE   You still alive, Bob Cratchit? You haven't died of pneumonia yet?

BOB CRATCHIT   Well I'm very cold, it's true, Mr. Scrooge. Might we put another coal on the fire?

EBENEZER SCROOGE   No we may not. I am not made of money, Bob Cratchit. A little cold never hurt anyone.

BOB CRATCHIT   I have this sort of pain right in the middle of my chest every time I breathe in the cold air.

EBENEZER SCROOGE   Really? Well when you're about to fall over dead, tell me, so I can go out and hire your replacement.

BOB CRATCHIT   Yes, sir. Oh, Mr. Scrooge, there are two gentlemen to see you, sir.

EBENEZER SCROOGE   What did I tell you about letting people wait for me in my office?

BOB CRATCHIT   You said not to do it.

EBENEZER SCROOGE   And so why did you do it?

BOB CRATCHIT   I have trouble saying no to people, Mr. Scrooge.

EBENEZER SCROOGE   Slap yourself in the face, Bob Cratchit.

BOB CRATCHIT   I'd rather not, Mr. Scrooge.

EBENEZER SCROOGE   Don't say no to me.

BOB CRATCHIT   Very well, sir.

Bob Cratchit slaps himself in the face.

EBENEZER SCROOGE   Ah, very good. I knew there was some reason I paid you your tiny weekly salary.

BOB CRATCHIT   And why is that, sir?

EBENEZER SCROOGE   You amuse me. Hit yourself again.

Bob hits himself again.

Oh very good. You're starting to put me in a good mood. Now, let me go be abusive to the gentlemen in my office.

Scrooge goes into his office area. The two gentlemen speak to him.

GENTLEMAN 1   Good morning, Mr. Scrooge. Merry Christmas.

GENTLEMAN 2   Merry Christmas to you, sir.

EBENEZER SCROOGE   Bah humbug! I want to put bugs in your hair.

GENTLEMAN 1   What kind of bugs, sir?

EBENEZER SCROOGE   Oh, disgusting horrible ones who'll emit some sort of terrible liquid all over your heads. Hahahahaha. And people say I don't have a sense of humor. What is it you want today, bah-humbug, Christmas-stinks-Christmas-carols-make-me-puke.

GENTLEMAN 2 (*aside to Gentleman 1*)   Goodness, if we lived in another century, I would say this man has Tourette's syndrome.

GENTLEMAN 1   Mr. Scrooge, we are fellow businessmen collecting for the United Way. And every Christmas we give a little bit from our pockets to all the poor people who wander throughout London in poverty and despair. And we wondered how much we could put you down for.

EBENEZER SCROOGE   Nothing.

GENTLEMAN 1   You wish to be anonymous?

EBENEZER SCROOGE   No, no, no—I wish to give nothing. Let the poor go to workhouses, or orphanages or die in the street. I am not my brother's keeper. I am a frugal businessman.

GENTLEMAN 1 Might you be interested in selling energy units with us?

EBENEZER SCROOGE Energy units?

GENTLEMAN 1 Mr. Scrooge, let me introduce myself. I'm Kenneth Lay, and this is my partner Jeffrey Skilling, doesn't he have a scary face? Now let me explain energy units.

Explains with energy and some speed.

You see, we take the warmth given off by the candle, say, and we "package" that energy, and then we set up a tax-free corporation in the Bahamas, and then we charge poor people, and the state of California, money for the use of these energy units. And we say there's a shortage and we triple the price, and we misstate our earnings and expenses, and our scribe Arthur Andersen shreds a lot of documents, and ultimately we make enormous profits without actually offering any services whatsoever. And then we all go bankrupt, and we retire as millionaires!

EBENEZER SCROOGE Gentlemen, I am extremely impressed. And I think I'd like to join in your business, and sell these "units of energy." Oh, Bob Cratchit, come in here a minute.

Bob Cratchit comes in.

BOB CRATCHIT Yes, Your Grace?

EBENEZER SCROOGE What is your weekly salary, Bob Cratchit?

BOB CRATCHIT You pay me eleven shillings, sir.

EBENEZER SCROOGE Well from now on I am paying you six shillings, Bob.

BOB CRATCHIT Why is that, sir?

EBENEZER SCROOGE I'm deducting five shillings from your salary, and purchasing some energy units for you and your family.

BOB CRATCHIT   Thank you, sir. And what are energy units so I may tell hardworking, exhausted Mrs. Cratchit when I see her next?

EBENEZER SCROOGE   Energy units, Bob, are like the warmth from a candle. I know how cold you say you always are, so I'm buying you some heat. And I'm charging you five shillings for it.

BOB CRATCHIT   Energy units and more warmth. Oh I think Mrs. Cratchit will be delighted to hear this, sir.

EBENEZER SCROOGE   Merry Christmas, Bob, hahaha, humbug, kaplooey.

BOB CRATCHIT   Yes, Mr. Scrooge, thank you very much.

Bob Cratchit goes back to his desk.

EBENEZER SCROOGE   Our first customer.

GENTLEMAN 1 (*offers his hand to Scrooge*)   Mr. Scrooge, I believe we've found a business partner.

EBENEZER SCROOGE   Merry Christmas! There, I can say it in celebration as long as it's a nasty thing I'm celebrating. Hooray for more money for me, and less for everybody else!

BOTH GENTLEMEN   Hear, hear, merry Christmas!

Lights dim on this scene. The Ghost comes downstage to speak.

GHOST   Wasn't that upsetting. And clearly Mr. Scrooge needs to be changed. So what shall we do next? Well, I think a little visit from his ex–business partner Jacob Marley may be in order, don't you? And some scary noises and some rattling chains. Coming right up.

SCENE 3

Scrooge's house.

A big wingback chair. Not much else. Maybe a clock on a wall. Enter Scrooge.

EBENEZER SCROOGE   Energy units, what a joke. Oh how I enjoy how stupid people are. Bob Cratchit, you and your children will freeze as much as always and I've cut your salary in half, and you'll thank me for it. Hahahaha. Bah humbug. Now let me sit in my favorite chair and read the announcements of the next public executions. (*sits in his chair, looks at a printed list*) Ah, next Tuesday, right after breakfast. I can make that one. Ah, my previous housekeeper, put to death for stealing. I will certainly make that one.

Offstage, the sound of some ghostly "woooo-ing."

OFF-STAGE GHOSTS   Woooooooo-ooooo.

EBENEZER SCROOGE   What is that, I wonder?

OFF-STAGE GHOSTS   Wooooooooo-oooooo!

EBENEZER SCROOGE   It must be my imagination.

Enter two ghosts, both dressed pathetically, with a "ghostly" sheet with a hole for their heads to poke through; and with a white piece of cloth wrapped from their chin to the top of their heads. Perhaps they both have socks with garters.

One ghost is the size of a man; the other is small, the size of a child.

They are JACOB MARLEY'S GHOST and YOUNG JACOB MARLEY from earlier, now dressed as a ghost.

THE MARLEY GHOSTS   Wooooooo-oooooo. Wooooooooooo-oooooo.

EBENEZER SCROOGE   Oh Lord, what is this?

JACOB MARLEY'S GHOST   Do you recognize me, Ebenezer?

EBENEZER SCROOGE   Not really.

JACOB MARLEY'S GHOST   Ebenezer, I am your business partner Jacob Marley, dead these many years.

EBENEZER SCROOGE   Well who dressed you, you look ridiculous.

JACOB MARLEY'S GHOST I am condemned to wander the earth, day after day, mourning my past mistakes, never to find rest or peace. (*emits a surprisingly loud cry of anguish*) OOOOOOOOOO-OOOOOOOOOOOOOOOOOOOHHHHHHHHHHHHHHH-HHHH!

YOUNG JACOB There, there, older self. Don't feel bad.

EBENEZER SCROOGE Is this young boy your servant?

JACOB MARLEY'S GHOST He is my tormentor!

EBENEZER SCROOGE He teases you?

JACOB MARLEY'S GHOST He torments me because I see how sweetly I began, and how empty and callous I ended.

EBENEZER SCROOGE Yes, yes, I see. I'm getting bored with your visit, can you leave?

JACOB MARLEY'S GHOST You are not afraid to speak to a ghost that way?

EBENEZER SCROOGE Well, are you a ghost? I think you could as easily be a piece of undigested mutton. Or some stomach-churning, unfinished glob of fermenting Rice-A-Roni.

YOUNG JACOB The San Francisco treat.

EBENEZER SCROOGE He has few lines, but enjoys the ones he has. Very good, young man, well spoken.

JACOB MARLEY'S GHOST (*emphatic, full of ghostly scariness*) Scrooooooooooge! I come with a warning. Unless you mend your ways, you will be condemned to the same fate as me—to walk the earth in torment for all your days. Wooooooooooooooo-ooooo, woe————

EBENEZER SCROOGE (*glib, wanting to be rid of him*) All right, fine, I'll change. Okay?

JACOB MARLEY'S GHOST Ebenezer, you will be visited three times tonight by three separate spirits—or possibly just one spirit, who will come three separate times and change its name each time. Either way, those spirits are your one and only chance to save yourself and escape your horrible fate.

EBENEZER SCROOGE Fine, fine, you've made your point. Please let me rest now.

JACOB MARLEY'S GHOST The first spirit will come when the clock strikes one. The second spirit will come when the clock strikes two. The third spir—

EBENEZER SCROOGE (*starts pushing them out*) Yes, yes, I get where you're going, thank you for coming. Goodbye, Jacob Marley. Goodbye, mini-Marley. Goodbye, goodbye, goodbye.

Scrooge gets the Marley Ghosts offstage. But immediately Jacob Marley's Ghost comes back.

JACOB MARLEY'S GHOST (*emphatic, needing to complete his thought*) The third spirit will come when the clock strikes three!!! (*glares, exits*)

Scrooge sits back in his chair, suddenly exhausted.

EBENEZER SCROOGE Oh, I am suddenly exhausted! How odd.

His body shifts abruptly, he suddenly nods off to a total sleep.

SCENE 4

Lights change. A clock strikes one. Scrooge opens his eyes.

EBENEZER SCROOGE Oh. The clock strikes one. Oh dear. I don't want to see a ghost.

Enter the Ghost. She is dressed as a UPS deliveryman.

GHOST UPS delivery. UPS delivery. Oh, Mr. Scrooge, I have a package.

EBENEZER SCROOGE Really? I was expecting a ghost. But a UPS delivery person is a welcome relief. What is it?

GHOST   A Christmas present from all your grateful friends and relatives.

She offers him a package . . . but wrapped like a festive Christmas gift, not like a UPS package.

EBENEZER SCROOGE   Really? That doesn't seem very likely. (*opens it*) Ah. A pair of socks. How fascinating. Bah, humbug!

GHOST   Mr. Scrooge, I am the Ghost of Christmas Past.

EBENEZER SCROOGE   And you're reduced to delivering packages?

GHOST   Yes, but with a purpose. Because I am here to teach you various lessons so you can improve your manner of keeping Christmas.

EBENEZER SCROOGE   Oh, you keep Christmas, leave me out of it.

GHOST   First of all, the way you receive presents is just no good. Try it again. (*offers him a second identical package*) Now before opening, you must proclaim in loud and grateful tones how lovely the wrapping is.

EBENEZER SCROOGE   I don't want to.

The Ghost reaches over with an electrical zapper and zaps him. Sound effect: Zap! Zap!

Aaaaaaaggggghh! What is that?

GHOST   That is an energy unit that we in the afterlife have fashioned into a zapper. And it zaps painful jolting electric currents through your body. And if you disobey, I shall use it again and again and again.

EBENEZER SCROOGE   Oh Lord.

GHOST   Now as I said, I want you to make a big fuss over the Christmas wrapping.

Scrooge stares at her with annoyance. She brandishes the zapper again.
He gives in, decides to do what she says.

EBENEZER SCROOGE (*with feigned, if slightly unconvincing, delight*)
Oh . . . what a lovely package. It is so, so very nice. Very, very,
very, very nice.

GHOST   Be more specific.

EBENEZER SCROOGE   It's so . . . colorful. I love the ribbon on it.
Ummm . . . what a lovely shade of yellow it is. Makes me think
of egg yolk, makes me think of vomit.

She zaps him.

Aaaaaaaaggghhhh! Makes me think of daffodils. Lovely, lovely
daffodils. What a wonderful package. I . . . I . . . hate even to
open it, it's so lovely.

GHOST   Much better. Now open it, and then gush about the gift.

EBENEZER SCROOGE   All right. (*while he starts to open it*) What do
you think is in it? It's too light to be a book. It's too small to be
a . . . cast-iron statue of Oliver Cromwell. What do you think it
is? Shall I see? (*opens it; takes out a pair of white gym socks*) Oh, how
marvelous! Socks! Just what I need. I love socks. Thank you so
very, very, very much.

GHOST   That was so-so. Gush some more.

EBENEZER SCROOGE   Ummmm. I love white socks. They're so
. . . clean. And useful. I'm thrilled out of my mind. Out of my
mind, I tell you. Is that enough? Can I stop talking about the
socks please???

GHOST   Yes, you may. For I am the Ghost of Christmas Past,
and we have visiting to do. First off, I think we shall go to the
Fezziwigs.

EBENEZER SCROOGE   Oh not those loud, awful bores.

GHOST The very ones. Come touch my arm and the set shall change around us.

EBENEZER SCROOGE Very well.

Scrooge touches the Ghost's arm, and there are air-rustling sounds, like racing through space and time. And the set changes around them and we find ourselves at:

SCENE 5

> *Bob Cratchit's house. A wooden table, missing a leg but standing nonetheless; it seats perhaps six. A chair or two. Mrs. Bob Cratchit is there, doing needlepoint. A couple of children lie on the floor, a girl and boy.*

> *Scrooge and the Ghost stand in the set, staring at them.*

CHILD 1 (*girl*) I'm hungry.

CHILD 2 (*boy*) Me too.

MRS. BOB CRATCHIT So we're all hungry. What do you want me to do about it?

CHILD 1 Give us some food.

EBENEZER SCROOGE This isn't the Fezziwigs.

GHOST You're right, it's not. I seem to have brought us to the wrong place.

MRS. BOB CRATCHIT Excuse me, who are you?

GHOST Uh . . . no one. I'm a ghost. You can't see me.

EBENEZER SCROOGE And I'm just some old man. (*whispers to Ghost*) Why can she see us?

GHOST I don't know, something's wrong. (*to Mrs. Bob Cratchit*) We were looking for the Fezziwigs.

MRS. BOB CRATCHIT Oh? And who might they be?

GHOST They were employers of Mr. Scroo . . . of this old gentleman long ago. Tell me, is this the present or the past?

MRS. BOB CRATCHIT Every day of my life seems the same to me, I haven't a clue if it's the present or the past. Children, are we in the present or the past?

CHILD 1 I'm hungry.

CHILD 2 Feed us!

MRS. BOB CRATCHIT All children want to do is eat, it's disgusting. (*screams at them*) WHEN YOUR FATHER FINALLY MAKES SOME MONEY, THEN YOU'LL EAT! AND NOT A MINUTE BEFORE!

GHOST Oh right, this is Bob Cratchit's house, isn't it?

MRS. BOB CRATCHIT What?

GHOST We're supposed to be here much later. Something's gone awry.

MRS. BOB CRATCHIT I'm sorry, who are you and why are you here?

GHOST (*to Scrooge*) Touch my cloak and I'll try to get us back in time to the Fezziwigs.

EBENEZER SCROOGE What cloak?

GHOST My arm then, don't be so fussy. Touch my arm.

Scrooge touches the Ghost's arm and there's a large POP sound. Brief flash of light too. Though Scrooge and the Ghost are still there.

MRS. BOB CRATCHIT Oh! Where did those two go? The black delivery woman and the old doddering man. Children, did you see them leave?

CHILD 1 I'm hungry.

MRS. BOB CRATCHIT Shut up. That's strange, I didn't see them leave.

GHOST Well at least we're invisible now. That part is working again. Touch my arm again, and I'll try to get us to the Fezziwigs.

Scrooge touches her arm. Nothing.

Damn it, I don't know what's the matter.

MRS. BOB CRATCHIT Children, don't swear.

GHOST We're here at the Cratchit house way too early.

CHILD 2 Father and Tiny Tim are home, I think.

MRS. BOB CRATCHIT I wonder what good news your father will have for Christmas Eve. Maybe Scrooge will have died and named us in his will, ha ha ha.

EBENEZER SCROOGE That's rather rude.

MRS. BOB CRATCHIT (*to the children*) Did you say something?

CHILD 1 No. We didn't say anything.

MRS. BOB CRATCHIT I thought I heard a voice. Oh Lord, I'm hearing things now.

EBENEZER SCROOGE Can they hear us?

GHOST They're not supposed to.

Enter Bob Cratchit and Tiny Tim. Bob has a long, long scarf around his neck that falls to the ground. Tiny Tim is small, carries a little crutch, and limps a lot.

BOB CRATCHIT Gladys, darling, we're home. And Tiny Tim so enjoyed looking in the store windows at all the Christmas treats he can't have.

TINY TIM And I only fell on the ground twenty-four times today.

MRS. BOB CRATCHIT Why won't you use your crutch, you stupid child?

TINY TIM I don't want to people to notice I'm crippled.

MRS. BOB CRATCHIT And if you fall down twenty-four times, you don't think they'll notice?

TINY TIM Leave me alone.

BOB CRATCHIT Let poor Tiny Tim alone, dear. He's a sensitive soul.

MRS. BOB CRATCHIT That damn crutch cost half of your weekly salary, and the idiot child won't use it.

TINY TIM I don't need it!

GHOST Isn't this a sad family? Do you feel sorry for them?

MRS. BOB CRATCHIT Did you hear that?

BOB CRATCHIT Hear what, my darling?

MRS. BOB CRATCHIT I heard some voice saying we're a sad family.

BOB CRATCHIT Oh, and so we are, and proud of it. I see the people on the street point at me and Tiny Tim, and they say, "Look, there goes that man who hasn't money to feed his twenty children, and there's his little cripple child. But he's a kind man," they say.

MRS. BOB CRATCHIT If we have so little money, why do you keep adopting children?

BOB CRATCHIT I love children. Where are the children?

MRS. BOB CRATCHIT They're all in a bunch in the root cellar.

Bob Cratchit opens a trapdoor and calls down to presumably a horde of children.

BOB CRATCHIT Merry Christmas, children! I hope you're all well and happy!

MANY VOICES (*perhaps recorded on tape; in unison*) We're hungry!

CHILD 1 AND CHILD 2 We're hungry too!

BOB CRATCHIT Children are always so hungry, it's kind of cute. Oh, my Lord, I forgot. . . .

Bob Cratchit runs to the main door, and goes out it.

TINY TIM Father has a Christmas surprise for you, Mother.

Bob Cratchit comes running back in with a bundle, wrapped in a blanket.

BOB CRATCHIT Look, darling, another foundling. I found a foundling.

MRS. BOB CRATCHIT And what do you want me to do with it? Cook it for Christmas dinner in place of the goose we don't have?

CHILD 1 AND CHILD 2 We're hungry. Feed us!

MRS. BOB CRATCHIT We're not cannibals yet, children. Soon, but not yet.

EBENEZER SCROOGE Oh what a gruesome family.

MRS. BOB CRATCHIT Did you hear that?

BOB CRATCHIT Hear what?

MRS. BOB CRATCHIT Someone said we were gruesome.

BOB CRATCHIT I didn't hear anything.

MRS. BOB CRATCHIT Maybe I'm losing my mind. That would be a nice Christmas present.

GHOST We really should be at the Fezziwigs.

MRS. BOB CRATCHIT Bob Cratchit, we already have twenty other children, all of whom have to sleep in a great big pile in the root cellar and rarely have enough to eat. Are you out of your mind, bringing another child into this house?

Bob Cratchit hands the bundle to Mrs. Bob Cratchit.

BOB CRATCHIT   But you so love children, my darling.

MRS. BOB CRATCHIT   Love children? Are you stupid as well as poor? (*to the two children on the ground*) Children, do I act like I like children?

CHILD 1 AND CHILD 2   No, Mother.

TINY TIM   Indeed she does not. Mother often tears at her hair and cries out, "Oh what a wretched life I lead with twenty children."

MRS. BOB CRATCHIT   And now twenty-one! (*stands and screams*) God, strike me dead now, I don't want to live.

EBENEZER SCROOGE   Goodness. Why are you showing me this?

GHOST   I have no idea.

MRS. BOB CRATCHIT   Bob Cratchit, did you ask that horrible Mr. Scrooge for a raise as I told you to?

BOB CRATCHIT   Well an amusing story about that . . . I was going to, when Mr. Scrooge called me in and told me that he was buying us all energy units of heat out of half of my existing salary.

MRS. BOB CRATCHIT   What? Energy units of heat? And he's using HALF of your salary to buy whatever these things are? I may go mad right now. I'll go nuts, I'll go crackers.

CHILD 1   I want a cracker.

CHILD 2   I want a cracker.

BOB CRATCHIT   Listen to the children, they're so cute.

GHOST   Poor Mrs. Cratchit. She's losing her mind due to your business practices.

EBENEZER SCROOGE   Oh pooey. If she ends up in Bedlam, that's her problem.

MRS. BOB CRATCHIT   I'm hearing voices talk about me. They say I'm ready for Bedlam. And I am too.

BOB CRATCHIT Oh there's not a saner woman in all of London.

MRS. BOB CRATCHIT You're missing part of your brain, aren't you? Open the root cellar door, would you?

Bob Cratchit opens the trapdoor again. Mrs. Bob Cratchit goes over to it and calls down to the children.

Children, here's a new little brother or sister for you. Give it a name and take care of it, would you?

Mrs. Bob Cratchit starts to toss the foundling down there, but Bob Cratchit stops her.

BOB CRATCHIT Gladys, darling, what are you doing? This is an infant. You mustn't throw it down to the cellar. We must cherish it.

MRS. BOB CRATCHIT Oh, right, cherish it. (*to the foundling*) Hello, little child. Cherish, cherish, cherish. (*hands Bob Cratchit the child*) Here, you cherish the child awhile, would you? I think I want to go get a drink at the pub and then jump off London Bridge. (*calls down to the root cellar*) Goodbye, children. Mother's going to jump off the bridge. Do as I say and not as I do. Have a nice Christmas dinner tomorrow.

TINY TIM Oh, Mummy, don't die!

MRS. BOB CRATCHIT Don't tell me what to do!

CHILD 1 AND CHILD 2 Mummy! Mummy!

MRS. BOB CRATCHIT Goodbye, everyone! I can't stand being alive one more second!

Mrs. Bob Cratchit rushes out of the house.

BOB CRATCHIT Gladys, please don't do this. It's Christmas Eve! It's a happy time.

TINY TIM Where's Mummy going? How can she leave me, her little crippled child? Not to mention the new foundling, the two children sitting over there, and the remaining children in the root cellar?

BOB CRATCHIT   Oh what a long question that was, Tiny Tim, and I have not an answer for you. Oh it breaks my heart. I think we all better cry for your unhappy lot. On the count of three, everybody weep. One, two, three.

Bob Cratchit, Tiny Tim, and the two Children all weep.

EBENEZER SCROOGE (*uncomfortable*)   Oh, Lord, they're crying.

Lights dim on the Cratchits. The Ghost and Scrooge walk to another part of the stage.

That was very pathetic. If I weren't so heartless, I would've been moved. But I wasn't. And why does he keep bringing children home when they have no money? And don't you agree, Mrs. Cratchit seems in serious trouble?

GHOST   I don't mean to be rigid, but we're supposed to go to the Fezziwigs FIRST, so you can be reminded of your cheerful, Dickensian boss who was so generous and full of life and showed us all the joyful side of Christmas. We're not supposed to have witnessed any of what we just saw, and I can't let it distract us.

EBENEZER SCROOGE   I think I should go back to bed, and you should go back to Ghost School or something.

Scrooge starts to walk away.

GHOST   Ebenezer Scrooge, you come back here. We have got to make you change your personality by the end of this evening. Now admittedly we've had trouble getting things off to a proper start, but you're not to go back to bed. Though perhaps going back to your residence might be right . . . maybe I can get my astral directions working again, and then we can move on to the Fezziwigs. They're usually quite an audience favorite, and there's no point in depressing everyone with that sour rendition of Mrs. Bob Cratchit which is nowhere to be found in Dickens.

EBENEZER SCROOGE Oh very well. Let's walk back to my place, shall we? What an idiotic ghost.

The Ghost zaps Scrooge as they both exit.

SCENE 6

A pub. Various people milling around. A BARTENDER. *Everyone is singing a carol. They kind of know they don't know it.*

EVERYONE (*sings*)
Good King Wenceslaus looked out
On the feast of Stephen
As the snow lay deep about
Duh duh duh and even
Duh duh the moon that night
When the wind was cru-el
Duh duh duh duh came in sight
Serving Christmas gru-uel . . .

Mrs. Bob Cratchit sort of explodes into the room.

MRS. BOB CRATCHIT I NEED A DRINK!

The Bartender gives her a shot of something, which she drinks quickly.

Hit me again! (*gulps the second shot down*) And again! (*gulps the third shot down*) Okay. I'll let it kick in, and then I'll want directions to London Bridge.

The Ghost and Scrooge suddenly arrive.

GHOST At last! And now—the Fezziwigs!

The Ghost and Scrooge look around. No Fezziwigs in sight.

Gosh darn it! Come on, get a move here, I demand to conjure up the FEZZIWIGS!

Great noise and commotion. Lights go out, and flash around. Everyone in the pub sort of scurries on- and offstage, clearly something is happening. Maybe the sounds of alarm bells ringing too.

When the lights settle back on, the set is more or less the same, except a Christmas tree has been brought on. . . . The people in the pub have put on different accents to their costumes—festive hats? Or Christmas tinsel around their necks, or something.

*And significantly—*MR. AND MRS. FEZZIWIG *are there. They are dressed and padded to look like a male and female Tweedle Dee and Tweedle Dum; they have bright orange wigs on, and look extremely "Dickensian" in a clichéd, over-the-top way.*

They are extremely cheerful and happy; they dominate the room.

MR. AND MRS. FEZZIWIG MERRY CHRISTMAS, ONE AND ALL, FROM YOUR FRIENDS AND EMPLOYERS, THE FEZZIWIGS!

MRS. FEZZIWIG And God bless us, everyone one!

MRS. BOB CRATCHIT Tiny Tim says that!

MRS. FEZZIWIG Tiny who?

Mrs. Bob Cratchit looks around confused. She's not sure where she is. She knows it's not quite the pub she walked into a minute ago, but she also knows she's a bit drunk, and doesn't know where she is.

MRS. BOB CRATCHIT Where am I, I wonder? Things looks different.

MR. FEZZIWIG It's time to stop work, everyone. You too, Ebenezer Scrooge, you too, Dick Wilkins. Everyone get ready to drink some Christmas punch, spiked with a little Christmas cheer, and get ready to dance a merry ol' dance with our two matrimonially available daughters.

The two matrimonially available FEZZIWIG DAUGHTERS *enter just now, and grin at everyone, very happy and very available.*

EBENEZER SCROOGE   Yes, it's good ol' Mr. Fezziwig. I recognize him indeed. I and Dick Wilkins were apprentices to him when we were young men.

GHOST   Thank goodness, we finally got here! It's the past. And I am the Ghost of Christmas Past, and that's where we are. Phew!!!

MRS. BOB CRATCHIT   Where's the Christmas punch? Give me some punch!

EBENEZER SCROOGE   Oh, Lord. Why is she here?

GHOST   I don't know. She shouldn't be here. It's some glitch or other. Just pay her no attention.

MRS. BOB CRATCHIT   Some glitch? Oh I'm hearing voices again. (*hits her head with her hand*) Shut up, shut up!

GHOST   The lesson for you to learn is about how well the Fezziwigs celebrate Christmas, and how they make it fun for their employees. Can you focus on that please?

EBENEZER SCROOGE   Well, I'll try.

MRS. BOB CRATCHIT   I need some punch please!

MR. FEZZIWIG   Get this woman some punch!

Someone hands Mrs. Bob Cratchit a glass of punch. She gulps it.

MRS. BOB CRATCHIT   Mmmmm, delicious. Good. Now as soon as I'm really drunk, I want to kill myself.

MR. FEZZIWIG   Ha ha ha, that's a dark bit of humor there, now now, killing oneself is for other days, not for Christmas, and not for Christmas Eve. Am I right, Mrs. Fezziwig?

MRS. FEZZIWIG   You're right, Mr. Fezziwig. Holidays are wonderful things. And Christmas is the most wonderful holiday of them all. And why is that, Mr. Fezziwig?

MR. FEZZIWIG   Well, I'll tell you, Mrs. Fezziwig.

The Fezziwigs are just so darn happy they can't but help to sing a song.

Mr. Fezziwig begins the song with gusto, and is then joined by Mrs. Fezziwig, and eventually by all the happy PARTYGOERS *except for Scrooge, the Ghost, and Mrs. Bob Cratchit. Toward the end, even Scrooge and the Ghost join in the singing. Mrs. Bob Cratchit never does, though, but initially stays over by the punch bowl in a distracted funk until later on the dance movements of the happy people start to push her around the stage haphazardly.*

(sings)
Be happy and perky
You're gonna eat turkey
Be snippy and snappy
'Cause Christmas is happy

Scream out, be elated
Eat up 'til you're sated
Be zestful and zingy and tangy and gay

MR. AND MRS. FEZZIWIG *(sing)*
Eat, drink, and be merry
Play games under mistletoe berry
Eat, drink, and be jolly
Run mad, hang some tinsel and holly
It's Christmas and we're glad
The opposite of sad
With joy we may go mad

MR. FEZZIWIG *(sings)*
See now, snow is falling,
The fiddler is calling
Outside, trees are frosted
Good God, I'm exhausted!

He holds his heart a bit, short of breath.

MRS. FEZZIWIG AND PARTYGOERS *(sing)*
Christmas, Christmas, Christmas!

Mrs. Fezziwig helps Mr. Fezziwig stand up straight again, and he sings the next part with renewed vigor.

MR. FEZZIWIG (*sings*)
Be lively and frisky
You're gonna drink whiskey

MRS. FEZZIWIG (*sings*)
Go marching and drumming
'Cause Christmas is coming

MR. FEZZIWIG (*sings*)
Get plastered and tipsy
And dance like a gypsy

MRS. FEZZIWIG (*sings*)
Be zestful and zingy and tangy and tingy
And puckish and pingy and gay

Scrooge has been having fond memories of his apprenticeship with the Fezziwigs, so he now joins in the singing as well, to the surprise of the Ghost, who figures, what the heck, she'll sing too.

MR. AND MRS. FEZZIWIG, PARTYGOERS, SCROOGE, AND GHOST
(*singing*)
Eat, drink, and be merry
Play games under mistletoe berry
Eat, drink, and be jolly
Run mad, hang some tinsel and holly
It's Christmas and we're glad
The opposite of sad
With joy we may go mad
'Cause we're filled with glee and joy and cheer
Christmas, Christmas, Christmas, Christmas, Christmas, Christmas, Christmas!

MR. FEZZIWIG   Oh my God, I'm having a heart attack.

Mr. Fezziwig falls to the ground. Mrs. Fezziwig gives her husband mouth-to-mouth resuscitation. Then pounds on his chest.

GHOST Oh my God. (*to Scrooge*) Did he die in the past?

EBENEZER SCROOGE I don't think so. I would've remembered, wouldn't I? I hope I would've.

MRS. FEZZIWIG It's all right, everyone, Mr. Fezziwig is coming back to life again.

MR. FEZZIWIG (*sitting up*) Oh, my goodness, that was a close one. Bring me some punch and pastry.

MRS. FEZZIWIG Yes, he needs his strength. Bring him alcohol and pastries right away. Oh every Christmas he nearly dies of a heart attack, but he just can't help but show people how to have a good time at Christmas.

GHOST Good, well that's the point I was hoping to make.

MRS. BOB CRATCHIT Okay, I'm ready to die now. Which way to London Bridge?

GHOST Now, Mrs. Cratchit, can you hear me?

MRS. BOB CRATCHIT Yes, you're in my head all right.

GHOST Now listen to me. You need Paxil or Zoloft. Are you on an antidepressant?

MRS. BOB CRATCHIT On a what?

GHOST Oh that's right, I'm ahead of myself again. Well, just go home to Mr. Cratchit. I'm trying to redeem this man here and you're part of his story. If you kill yourself, the story has an entirely different meaning.

MRS. BOB CRATCHIT Story? I don't know what you're talking about. Which way to the river?

EBENEZER SCROOGE Oh, let her kill herself, and I'll just go home to bed.

GHOST No! You will not go back to bed. You are on a journey and we're going to get it right. Now I've showed you your childhood, and I've showed you the Fezziwigs. . . .

EBENEZER SCROOGE You haven't shown me my childhood.

GHOST Yes, I have. Oh my God, I haven't?

Mrs. Bob Cratchit starts to creep out.

MRS. BOB CRATCHIT I'll find the river myself. Good night. everyone. Merry Christmas, see you in hell! (*exits*)

MRS. FEZZIWIG Did she say, "See you in hell"? That's a terrible Christmas greeting.

GHOST Oh God, we've got to go back and do his childhood. . . . Scrooge, hold my arm . . . we're going back, back, back . . .

Everyone onstage makes a woo-woo sound, the lights go strange, and we're back in time.

SCENE 7

Young Ebenezer and Young Jacob stand next to each other, as in the first scene. The Ghost and Scrooge watch them. No one else is onstage.

YOUNG JACOB (*singing*)
Hark the herald angels sing
Glory to the newborn king

YOUNG EBENEZER Bah! Humbug!

GHOST Young Ebenezer hated Christmas from an early age.

YOUNG EBENEZER It's too commercial! And it's icky and goody-goody. I hate it!

GHOST Poor Ebenezer grew up in an orphanage.

EBENEZER SCROOGE No, I didn't.

GHOST Yes, you did.

A man and a woman, the BEADLE *and the* BEADLE'S WIFE, *enter with a big pot and a big ladle. The Beadle holds the pot; his Wife holds the ladle.*

The Beadle and his Wife are played by the same actors who played Mr. and Mrs. Fezziwig, but they've taken off their red wigs and made a few other minor costume adjustments.

BEADLE   Come get your porridge, you ungrateful orphan children.

BEADLE'S WIFE   So-weeeee! So-weeeeeee! Come along, little piggies!

The Wife ladles porridge into bowls, which Young Ebenezer and Young Jacob hold out to her.

Here's glop for you, and glop for you. Now, choke on it!

Young Ebenezer and Young Jacob mime gobbling up their oatmeal.

GHOST   Isn't it sad? The poor, poor children in this horrible orphanage.

BEADLE   The children should be very grateful for the food we give them, isn't that so, Mrs. Fezziwig?

BEADLE'S WIFE   My name isn't Mrs. Fezziwig.

BEADLE   No, of course, it's not. It's something else. Mrs. Cratchit?

BEADLE'S WIFE   No, I can't remember what my name is, but it isn't Mrs. Cratchit. Oh look, one of the young boys is coming over to us.

Young Ebenezer walks over to the Beadle and holds out his empty bowl.

YOUNG EBENEZER   Please, sir . . . I want some more.

BEADLE   What???

YOUNG EBENEZER Please, sir . . . I want some . . . more?

EBENEZER SCROOGE None of this rings a bell.

GHOST Well it's your childhood.

EBENEZER SCROOGE I don't remember it.

GHOST Well, you've repressed it.

BEADLE'S WIFE He wants more!! Oliver Twist, you are an ungrateful child!

EBENEZER SCROOGE You see, she said another name. You've taken me to some other person's past, you incompetent fool.

GHOST She didn't say Oliver Twist. She said Ebenezer Scrooge.

EBENEZER SCROOGE I heard her say Oliver Twist.

BEADLE'S WIFE Ebenezer Scrooge, you are an ungrateful child. I don't know why I said Oliver Twist. Maybe the other child is Oliver Twist.

YOUNG JACOB No. I'm Jacob Marley.

BEADLE'S WIFE Jacob Marley . . . I don't remember having an orphan by that name here.

BEADLE I think you're Mrs. Fezziwig.

BEADLE'S WIFE Well I'm not. You're the Beadle and I'm Mrs. Beadle.

BEADLE If you say so.

EBENEZER SCROOGE (*to Ghost*) I think you don't know what you're doing.

GHOST Look, the point is, you were either an orphan or you weren't, but you had a tough life, it helped to make you the mean, mean man you became. Okay? Point made . . . let's not get hung up on whether all the details are exactly right or not. All right?

EBENEZER SCROOGE I think you're incompetent.

GHOST   Well I think you're mean and stingy and a terrible person. (*zaps him with the zapper*)

EBENEZER SCROOGE   Aaaaaaaaagggghhhh!

GHOST   And now that's the end of my tenure as the Ghost of Christmas Past. You go back to sleep for a while, and the Ghost of Christmas Present will show up shortly.

BEADLE   And where do we go?

GHOST   You go to the kitchen, to wash out that disgusting pot.

BEADLE   All right.

BEADLE'S WIFE   Let's make the children wash the pot! And scrub the floor too!

YOUNG EBENEZER   I don't want to scrub the floor!

BEADLE'S WIFE   Oliver Twist, you're a lazy bum. You'll be fired from your first job.

YOUNG EBENEZER   Not if I'm self-employed I won't be.

BEADLE'S WIFE   Shut up!

The Beadle and his Wife exit, followed by Young Ebenezer and Young Jacob.

GHOST   Mininons of the night, send Mr. Scrooge back to sleep.

Ghost exits. Lights, music. A couple of "MINIONS OF THE NIGHT"—or townsfolk—help with the set change and move Scrooge back to his "home." Scrooge's chair comes back. The minions push Scrooge to it, and he sits in it.

If you like, the minions can be stagehands, dressed in their normal clothes.

MINIONS OF THE NIGHT   One o'clock, one o'clock, one forty-five. Scrooge is sleepy, Scrooge is sleepy.

Note: "One o'clock, one o'clock" is in rhythm of "patty cake, patty cake."

EBENEZER SCROOGE Why yes, I believe I am. (*falls asleep abruptly*)

MINIONS OF THE NIGHT Sleep in your chair. We don't have a set for the bed. Fall back asleep.

The minions exit.

SCENE 8

Scrooge back in his chair. He nods asleep. The clock strikes two. He awakens abruptly.

EBENEZER SCROOGE Two dings from the clock. That means two A.M. and a second spirit. But here I am in my chair, and all is well. I'm just having bad dreams, clearly. All that stuff about Jacob Marley and the Ghost of Christmas Past. It's just a dream.

Enter the Ghost again. Lights, magic music.

The Ghost is now out of her UPS costume. She is in some big robe, with a garland of Christmas-y greens on her head. She also has a pretty fake-looking beard on.

She's now the Ghost of Christmas Present; and in movies that figure is often presented as a jolly, bearded man with a fancy robe.

GHOST Ho, ho, ho! Ha, ha, ha! I am the Ghost of Christmas Present!

EBENEZER SCROOGE Oh God. I've had enough of this.

GHOST Ebenezer Scrooge, you are being given this opportunity to improve yourself.

EBENEZER SCROOGE All right, all right. Why do you have a beard now?

GHOST I don't know, I'm Father Christmas.

The Ghost takes off the beard, a bit annoyed with it.

Here, touch my cloak, we are to look at the ways in which touching, small people celebrate Christmas all over the world.

EBENEZER SCROOGE   Little lessons. I'm not a four year old.

GHOST   Mr. Scrooge, look at this lovely Dutch couple.

Enter MR. and MRS. DUTCH COUPLE. Mrs. Dutch is bald. They have strong Dutch accents.

MR. DUTCH PERSON   Merry Christmas, Mrs. Johanson.

MRS. DUTCH PERSON   Merry Christmas, my darling husband. Even though we have no money, I have managed to buy you a Christmas gift, darling Edvar. Look—a watch fob for the cherished timepiece that your father gave you.

MR. DUTCH PERSON (*bit disappointed*)   Oh thank you.

MRS. DUTCH PERSON   You don't like it?

MR. DUTCH PERSON   I like it very much, it's just . . . well, I'm afraid I sold my watch to pay for my present for you.

GHOST (*to Scrooge*)   I hope you're taking this in?

EBENEZER SCROOGE   Why is she bald?

GHOST   I don't know, be quiet.

MRS. DUTCH PERSON   Oh, Edvar, you bought me a Christmas gift by selling your watch. I am so touched. What did you get me?

MR. DUTCH PERSON   I got you a beautiful comb to wear in your lovely hair. (*hands her the comb; looks at her*) Oh my God! Where is your hair???

MRS. DUTCH PERSON   Oh, Edvar. I sold my hair in order to buy you a Christmas present.

MR. DUTCH PERSON   You sold your hair that you love and value more than life itself?

MRS. DUTCH PERSON   Yes, I did.

MR. DUTCH PERSON   Oh, Hedvig! This is so tragic!

MRS. DUTCH PERSON   Oh, Edvar! It is. We've both given up things we love in order to buy presents which are now useless. How I hate Christmas.

MR. DUTCH PERSON   I hate Christmas too, Hedvig. Come, let us go into the other room and kill ourselves.

MRS. DUTCH PERSON   I'd love to. But I sold my father's gun last year to buy you arrows, don't you remember?

MR. DUTCH PERSON   Oh right. Except I could not use the arrows because I had sold the bow to buy a copper bracelet for your arthritis.

MRS. DUTCH PERSON   And, of course, I don't have arthritis. Darling, wait! We still have the arrows! Why don't we impale ourselves on them as a way of dying?

MR. DUTCH PERSON   Marvelous idea!

GHOST   Stop, stop, stop. This is all wrong! Go away, go away. (*pushes the two people off*) That's not the proper story. I knew something was wrong when their names were Edvar and Hedvig. That story isn't about suicidal Dutch people.

EBENEZER SCROOGE   It was a good story though. And I agree with the meaning—Christmas is stupid and makes us do stupid, awful things.

GHOST   Oh Lord . . . no, that's wrong. (*zaps him with zapper*)

EBENEZER SCROOGE   Aaaaaaaaaggggghhhhh!

GHOST   Now forget everything they said, would you? Oh God. This isn't going like it's supposed to. Okay, we've done Fezziwig, we went back and sort of did your childhood, we've seen Christmas celebrated 'round the world. NOW is when we're supposed to go to Bob Cratchit's house.

EBENEZER SCROOGE   Oh not the Cratchits again. I'm going to fire that man first thing in the morning, I never want to see him again.

GHOST   You may not live through the morning. Now touch my cloak.

EBENEZER SCROOGE   The Cratchits. What a bunch of crap.

GHOST   Shut up.

SCENE 9

The Cratchit house arrives back. Still the table with three legs. There is a pathetic Christmas tree—tiny, few limbs, with like three Christmas balls hung on it and a few strands of tinsel on one branch.

Bob Cratchit is singing a carol with the children—Tiny Tim, and Child 1 and Child 2. It's "Silent Night." They are singing it at a normal, slightly slow tempo.

BOB CRATCHIT AND CHILDREN (*singing*)
Silent night, holy night
All is calm

BOB CRATCHIT (*spoken*)   Sing it slower, children. Drag it out.

BOB CRATCHIT AND CHILDREN (*singing, really slowly*)
All is bright
Round yon virgin
Mother and child

EBENEZER SCROOGE (*spoken, during the singing above*)   Oh God, make them stop that.

GHOST   It's a beloved Christmas song.

BOB CRATCHIT AND CHILDREN (*singing, dirgelike*)
Holy infant
So tender and mild . . .

EBENEZER SCROOGE (*during the above, after a bit*)   It's driving me mad! Faster, faster!

BOB CRATCHIT AND CHILDREN (*singing, slowly*)
Sleep in heavenly pe-eace . . .

BOB CRATCHIT (*speaks again*)   Very, very slow now, children . . .

BOB CRATCHIT AND CHILDREN (*all sing again, slo-o-wly*)
Slee-eep in heavenly peeeeeeeeeeeeeeeeeece.

> As the song drags on, Scrooge should feel free to emit noises of enormous frustration: yelps and little screams. As well as to do some angry finger snapping and moving of hands to demand faster tempo.

EBENEZER SCROOGE (*during the last notes, clutches his ears and calls out*)   Make it end, make it end!

> *The song finishes.*

Oh thank God.

BOB CRATCHIT   Shall we sing it again, children?

CHILDREN   Oh yes, Father!

EBENEZER SCROOGE   NOOOOOOOOOOO!

> *Scrooge rushes at Bob Cratchit and knocks him off his chair to the ground.*

GHOST   Mr. Scrooge!

TINY TIM   Father, are you all right?

BOB CRATCHIT   Yes. Something pushed me out of my chair, that's all.

TINY TIM   I hope you're not going to be crippled like me.

BOB CRATCHIT   That's sweet of you to worry, Tiny Tim. You're a sensitive child.

TINY TIM   If we were both crippled, people might not know which one of us to feel sorry for.

CHILD 1 Well then they could feel sorry for both of you.

TINY TIM That's true. But they might go into sympathetic overdrive, and then start to avoid us.

BOB CRATCHIT Well, Tiny Tim, it's sweet of you to obsess about it, but really I'm not crippled, I just fell down and went b'm.

Note: Pronounced like "boom," but with a shorter vowel sound . . . somewhere between "boom" and "bum." B'm. The traditional way parents say it to children, but how do you spell that?

CHILDREN (*delighted*) B'm! B'm!

Enter LITTLE NELL. *She is a big girl—either tall and big or even heavy. She carries a large bag in which she hides some gifts, we will find out.*

She's sensitive, like Tiny Tim. But also has a bit of a hale and hearty, "look on the bright side" attitude. So she has energy.

LITTLE NELL Hello, Father. Hello, Tiny Tim. Hello, other two children.

BOB CRATCHIT Look, children, it's your older sister Little Nell, home from the sweatshop. Did you bring home your pitiful salary to help us pay the bills?

LITTLE NELL I was going to, dearest Father, but then on the street I saw such a pathetic sight. A woman of indeterminate age, shivering in the cold and clutching her starving children. They were weeping and rending their garments. And because it's Christmastime, I felt such a tender feeling in my heart that I just had to give all my salary to them.

BOB CRATCHIT That's lovely to hear, Little Nell. Children, your sister gives us all a good example.

LITTLE NELL But I had saved enough money from before, with my nighttime job of selling matches in the snow, that I've been able to buy everyone presents.

TINY TIM   Presents, presents! Oh my little heart may burst!

GHOST   You see how happy and touching they are?

EBENEZER SCROOGE   If you say so. Just promise me they won't sing "Silent Night" again.

LITTLE NELL   Would anyone like to sing "Silent Night" with me?

EBENEZER SCROOGE   NOOOOOOO!!!!

Scrooge rushes at Little Nell and pushes her off her stool. She falls to the ground.

LITTLE NELL   Aaaaaaaaaaggghhh! What was that???

GHOST   Mr. Scrooge, stop that!

BOB CRATCHIT   Just a very strong wind in here, darling Little Nell. I like your sweater, is it new?

LITTLE NELL   Yes, Father. I made it myself at the sweatshop from extra yarn and table scraps that fell on the floor. It's my little gift to myself to keep my spirits up.

BOB CRATCHIT   Well it's even nicer than your earlier sweater that your mother made a stew out of. (*suddenly realizing, worried*) Children, where is your mother?

TINY TIM   I don't know, Father. We haven't seen her for several hours since she said she was going to jump off the London Bridge.

LITTLE NELL   Oh my gracious.

CHILD 1 AND CHILD 2   Mummy, Mummy! We want Mummy!

BOB CRATCHIT   Come, children, let us pray for the safe return of Mrs. Cratchit.

TINY TIM   What if she's dead? Think how pathetic I'll be then!

GHOST   Oh my God, I can't have Mrs. Cratchit be dead. Wait, I'm going to need all my powers.

The Ghost spreads her arms, with firm authority. Bright light hits her and she intones.

Hear me, spirits and ghosts around us. By all the powers vested in me from heaven and above, I call upon the forces of the wind and sea to bring Mrs. Bob Cratchit back to her proper home right now!

Sounds of wind; then nothing.

Nothing? Okay, what if I do this?

With a bit of "I hate when I have to stoop to trying this"; sings

Camptown ladies
Sing this song
Do da, do da
Camptown races . . .

Mrs. Bob Cratchit, her clothes and hair looking wet, comes dancing into the room, suddenly singing the fourth line along with the Ghost. It's as if the song has magically called her back from the river.

MRS. BOB CRATCHIT (*singing*)
Camptown races
All day long
Oh de do day day!

She suddenly sees where she is and screams.

Aaaaaaaaaaaaaaaaggghhh!!!!

GHOST It worked!

MRS. BOB CRATCHIT NO NO NO!

CHILDREN Mummy! Mummy!

TINY TIM Merry Christmas, Mother. And God bless us, everyone.

MRS. BOB CRATCHIT No, I don't want to be here.

BOB CRATCHIT Gladys, are you all right?

MRS. BOB CRATCHIT Wait a minute.

She struggles inside her bodice; something is moving around that is bothering her.

Uh . . . uh . . . got it!

From inside her bodice she brings out a big fish.

Look, children, straight from the filthy, stinking Thames River. Mother's brought home a fish. How'd you all like fish for Christmas dinner?

TINY TIM No thank you very much. I would prefer a Christmas goose and huckleberries and candied yams and then Mother's special Christmas pudding.

MRS. BOB CRATCHIT Well you're gonna eat sushi and like it. Here, start nibbling on it now!

She hands him the fish.

EBENEZER SCROOGE Spirit, why did you bring this woman back? She clearly was happier at the bottom of the river.

GHOST Mr. and Mrs. Cratchit are part of the story. They're very poor and they're BOTH very sweet. Now from now on, Mrs. Cratchit will behave correctly.

The Ghost waves her hand toward Mrs. Bob Cratchit, as if she has power to change her.

MRS. BOB CRATCHIT (*sweetly*) Hello, children. Hello, Bob. Hello, Tiny Tim. Mother's home now, Merry Christmas.

LITTLE NELL Oh look, Mother is her old self again.

MRS. BOB CRATCHIT (*sweetly*) That's right, Little Nell. (*suddenly looks at Little Nell*) What's that hideous thing you're wearing?

GHOST Oh dear. Something's wrong with Mrs. Cratchit again.

The Ghost waves her hand again at Mrs. Bob Cratchit, but Mrs. Bob Cratchit brushes it away like a mosquito.

MRS. BOB CRATCHIT   Little Nell, you stupid child, I've asked you a question.

LITTLE NELL   It's a new sweater I knit for myself at the sweatshop.

MRS. BOB CRATCHIT   You're so awful-looking. Haven't I told you repeatedly you look like a bowl of porridge?

LITTLE NELL   When you're the bad mommy you say that. But when you're the good mommy, you stroke my hair and say, "There, there, Little Nell, who cares if you're homely as long as your heart is pure."

MRS. BOB CRATCHIT   Well I'm the bad mommy now. YOU LOOK LIKE A BOWL OF OATMEAL! No one will ever marry you . . . or if you did find some sorry soul, he'd pour milk on you, sprinkle sugar on your head, and eat your face for breakfast.

Little Nell cries.

BOB CRATCHIT   Darling, must you continually tell Little Nell she looks like a bowl of oatmeal? She may not be the prettiest flower in the garden, but there's no need to rub her face in it.

MRS. BOB CRATCHIT   And why is she called Little Nell? She's enormous.

LITTLE NELL   Okay, well excuse me for living then. Why don't I just crawl into the gutter and die?

MRS. BOB CRATCHIT   Finally, a constructive suggestion!

EBENEZER SCROOGE   I like Mrs. Cratchit. Is that what I'm supposed to get from seeing this?

GHOST   Oh, God. No it isn't.

MRS. BOB CRATCHIT   Did anyone hear a voice?

BOB CRATCHIT   Your mother is hearing voices, children. We should say a prayer.

MRS. BOB CRATCHIT (*somewhat touched*)   I heard a voice saying they liked me. Gosh, I haven't heard anyone say they liked me in a long time. Ever, actually.

TINY TIM   I like you, Mother. I love you.

MRS. BOB CRATCHIT   Oh shut up. You're just hungry.

Tiny Tim, Little Nell, and the two other children weep and cry.

BOB CRATCHIT   Gladys, look, you've made the children cry. And on Christmas too.

MRS. BOB CRATCHIT   The children are always crying. Our life is so damnably pathetic. No food to eat, no coal for the stove . . . I just hate my life. Does everyone get it?

EBENEZER SCROOGE   She speaks up for herself. It's so unusual.

GHOST   She has a bad attitude.

EBENEZER SCROOGE   Indeed. That's why she's so delightful.

MRS. BOB CRATCHIT   Goodness. I just heard a voice calling me delightful. How unlike the voices I usually hear in my head.

LITTLE NELL   Why does Mother hate us, Father?

MRS. BOB CRATCHIT   Well look in the mirror, why don't you?

Little Nell weeps.

BOB CRATCHIT   Now, now, it's Christmastime. Only happy, loving thoughts and sentences.

TINY TIM   Mummy doesn't hate us. She's just grouchy 'cause she's all wet. I love you, Mummy. My heart is so filled with goodness I can only see your goodness.

MRS. BOB CRATCHIT   Well, isn't that nice?

BOB CRATCHIT (*trying to change the subject*)   I have an idea. Maybe it's time for us to open all the Christmas presents that Little Nell has for us.

Little Nell looks pleased.

TINY TIM   Oh yes, may we? Please, please!

CHILD 1 AND CHILD 2   Presents, presents!

LITTLE NELL   Ssssssh, not too loud. I didn't have enough money to buy presents for all the children in the root cellar, I don't want them to hear.

TINY TIM (*whispers*)   Okay, we'll be quiet.

LITTLE NELL   Father, a present for you. Mother, a present for you. Precious Tiny Tim, a special present for you.

TINY TIM   Oooooooohhhh!

LITTLE NELL   Child One and Child Two, a present each for you. And . . . I wish I had another gift to offer to a certain "spirit" I sense in the room.

BOB CRATCHIT   A spirit?

LITTLE NELL   I just had a sense an "otherworldly presence" was here.

TINY TIM   Oooooh, she's scaring me.

BOB CRATCHIT   Now, now, don't be frightened. I don't think there are such things as ghosts and spirits. But you may offer it my present if you like.

LITTLE NELL   I'd like to see if the Ghost would take it from my hand.

Bob Cratchit gives Little Nell his present.

EBENEZER SCROOGE   Can she see you?

GHOST   I don't think so. It's very confusing. They're not supposed to hear or see me, but it keeps going ka-plooey.

MRS. BOB CRATCHIT   Ka-plooey.

LITTLE NELL (*holding out the present*)   Oh Ghost, I'm going to let go of the gift now. If you're there, let me see you catch it and make it float around the room.

Little Nell lets go of the present. It drops to the floor. Nothing happens.

Oh. Perhaps no one's there.

Scrooge mischievously picks up the present and carries it around the room. The Cratchits, one and all, scream.

THE CRATCHITS   Aaaaaaaaaaaaaaaagggghhhh!

Scrooge moves the present all over the room in intricate ways. The Cratchits keep screaming. He especially goes out of his way to scare Tiny Tim, keeps waving the present in his face.

Finally, annoyed, the Ghost grabs the present from Scrooge.

GHOST   Stop that!

The Ghost throws the present to the ground, and stomps on it repeatedly.

The Cratchits stop screaming. Little Nell looks hurt and horrified.

LITTLE NELL   Look how it's destroyed the present. Oh, it's so sad.

BOB CRATCHIT   Well that's but one present. I don't need one. And by my count, Little Nell still has presents for the rest of you.

OTHER CHILDREN   Hooray, hooray!

Tiny Tim, Child 1, Child 2, and Mrs. Bob Cratchit all receive presents from Little Nell. The children look at theirs in wonderment, they're so prettily wrapped.

GHOST   You see how generous Bob Cratchit is? He thinks of others.

MRS. BOB CRATCHIT   "Generous" indeed. He just has this image of himself as noble and good, he's so good out of puffed-up self-regard.

BOB CRATCHIT What?

MRS. BOB CRATCHIT Nothing. I'm concentrating on the presents.

The children start to unwrap their presents. Mrs. Bob Cratchit weighs hers in her hand.

Well, it's certainly light enough. What is it, a meringue?

They all unwrap their presents. Under the festive wrapping, there are cardboard boxes. They open their boxes, and look inside.

TINY TIM They're empty!

CHILD 1 There's nothing in them.

MRS. BOB CRATCHIT Yes, that's what "empty" means.

LITTLE NELL I didn't have much money. I spent what I had on the Christmas wrapping.

TINY TIM (*disappointed, but covering politely*) Oh. Well the wrapping was very nice. I wish I hadn't torn it up.

MRS. BOB CRATCHIT Little Nell. Next time you buy presents, actually buy presents. Don't just give us empty boxes, you idiot child!

LITTLE NELL I didn't have enough money for presents.

MRS. BOB CRATCHIT Well then you take the little money you have, and you buy something small and then you DON'T WRAP IT. Or you GIVE us the money directly.

LITTLE NELL I thought you'd like the wrapping.

MRS. BOB CRATCHIT Well I didn't!

EBENEZER SCROOGE Ghost of Christmas Present, why are you showing me this?

GHOST I don't know. I'm confused.

TINY TIM   Mummy, isn't it time for Christmas dinner? For the Christmas goose and the huckleberries and the candied yams and then the Christmas pudding?

MRS. BOB CRATCHIT   Children, I've been out drinking and trying to drown myself in the Thames—you think I have time to be cooking for you??? God, when will feminism be invented so people won't just assume I'll be cooking all the time, and be positive and pleasant. I wish this were 1977, then I'd be admired for my unpleasantness!

EBENEZER SCROOGE   1977 sounds interesting. I wonder if they'd like me there too?

GHOST   The two of you are impossible. I don't know how to make you learn the lesson of Christmas.

The Ghost zaps Scrooge.

EBENEZER SCROOGE   Aaaaaaaagggh!

The Ghost zaps Mrs. Bob Cratchit.

MRS. BOB CRATCHIT   Aaaaaaaaggghhh! (*looks around accusingly at everyone*) Who did that? Who did that?

BOB CRATCHIT   Did what, darling?

MRS. BOB CRATCHIT   Somebody did something to my arm.

LITTLE NELL   I thought people would like the wrapping.

BOB CRATCHIT   Now, now, let it go, Little Nell.

TINY TIM   So am I to assume there is no Christmas dinner?

MRS. BOB CRATCHIT   Yes, that's what you're to "assume." Why does he talk this way? Is he a British child?

BOB CRATCHIT   Yes, darling, we're all British.

MRS. BOB CRATCHIT   Really? I feel like I'm from Cleveland.

Well, never mind. No, Tiny Tim, there's no dinner. We can eat the dust on the floor.

Child 2 stands, proud to make an announcement.

CHILD 2 Mummy, Daddy, Tiny Tim. I have a surprise. While Mummy was in the river, I was in the kitchen—and I cooked the dinner.

THE OTHER CHILDREN Ooooooooooh!!! Christmas dinner!

BOB CRATCHIT Child Number Two, you're so good. Gladys, maybe it's time we gave him a name.

MRS. BOB CRATCHIT Okay. (*names him:*) Martha.

CHILD 2 But I'm a boy.

MRS. BOB CRATCHIT Okay. Marthum.

CHILD 2 Marthum?

BOB CRATCHIT It's all right, dear, your mother's difficult, just be glad she called you anything.

MRS. BOB CRATCHIT That's right. I'm very difficult. But then life is difficult.

BOB CRATCHIT Gladys, darling. Please look on the bright side once in a while. Our lovely child Marthum has cooked us Christmas dinner. Isn't that nice? Isn't that worth being happy about?

MRS. BOB CRATCHIT (*thinks; wants to be negative, but can't think how to spin it bad*) Yes, but . . .

BOB CRATCHIT Yes, but what, darling?

MRS. BOB CRATCHIT Yes, but . . . well, I suppose I could be glad about it. It is very nice we can have Christmas dinner, and I didn't have to make it. (*warning*) Although I don't want to do dishes afterward.

TINY TIM I'll do the dishes, precious Mummy.

MRS. BOB CRATCHIT You always drop the dishes. Although it makes me laugh when you do.

BOB CRATCHIT Yes, Tiny Tim's so awkward, sometimes it's fun to laugh at him. I mean, with him.

Tiny Tim smiles happily.

MRS. BOB CRATCHIT All right. I admit it. I'm feeling better. Marthum, thank you for cooking, now perhaps you could go and get the dinner.

CHILD 2 Can't we sing a song about dinner first?

MRS. BOB CRATCHIT Oh God, what's all this singing all the time?

BOB CRATCHIT It's Christmas, darling. There are carols and hymns and original songs written directly for us, like this next one.

MRS. BOB CRATCHIT Well all right. I can be in a good mood occasionally.

BOB CRATCHIT And then after the song, a short intermission so we can use the loo, and then delicious Christmas dinner right after the interval.

Bob Cratchit, Mrs. Bob Cratchit, Tiny Tim, Little Nell, and the two other children all sing "The Christmas Dinner Song." It's cheerful and hearty, like a German drinking song; kind of like a celebratory song from Oliver.

BOB CRATCHIT, MRS. BOB CRATCHIT, TINY TIM, LITTLE NELL, CHILD 1, AND CHILD 2 (*singing*)
Eat drink
Yummy yum yum
At Christmas each year
We fill our tum tum
Chew up
And savor the meal

At Christmas each year
With pleasure we squeal
Yay, yay, yay, yay!★
Our joy is contagious, our laughter profuse,
The berries and pudding, the yams and the goose!

Sip, slurp
Yummy yum yum

TINY TIM, CHILD 1, AND CHILD 2 *(singing)*
We like to get drunk
On egg nog and rum

BOB CRATCHIT, MRS. BOB CRATCHIT, TINY TIM, LITTLE NELL,
CHILD 1, AND CHILD 2 *(singing)*
Chow down
Some morsel of pork

LITTLE NELL *(singing)*
We grab with our hands
We don't use a fork

BOB CRATCHIT, MRS. BOB CRATCHIT, TINY TIM, LITTLE NELL,
CHILD 1, AND CHILD 2 *(singing)*
Yay, yay, yay, yay!
It gets kind of messy, the jellies and jams
The berries and pudding, the goose and the yams!

TINY TIM
Bless us all
Our tummies fill
Though I'm small
My belly will
Accept all pies
Served a la mode
I'll stuff them down
'Til I explode

★"Yay" rhymes with "say."

He puffs out his cheeks, indicates stomach exploding.

*The Ghost prods Scrooge and makes him join the song. So this next
section is sung by everyone, the Ghost and Scrooge as well. Mrs. Bob
Cratchit can play she hears additional voices if she wants—though that
may be too busy to work.*

EVERYONE (*singing*)
Gulp, gorge
Be glutonous too
Each swallow you take
Each mouthful you chew
Swig, swill
And drink lots of beer
Get drunk and fall down
It's Christmas, my dear
Yum, yum, yum, yum
We're covered with gravy and cranberry juice
Too good to eat slowly, so that's our excuse
The berries and pudding, the yams and the goose!
Yum yum!

The song ends triumphantly.

End Act 1.

ACT 2

SCENE 9 (cont.)

The Cratchit family is seated around the dinner table. The table has a large swan on it made of plastic or papier-mâché. And the Christmas pudding is very, very large and black, and does look like the traditional English Christmas pudding.

The Cratchits are frozen in a tableau at the top.

The Ghost addresses the audience in a spot. Scrooge stands near her, but is not in the spot. He is not frozen. He's eating a Popsicle.

GHOST (*sings to audience; a bit sassy*)
Ta Ra Ra, Boom De Ay
That's what some people say
When they begin their day
And they come out to play

Ta Ra Ra, Boom De Ay
Ta Ra Ra, Boom De Ay
Ta Ra Ra, Boom De Ay
Ta Ra Ra, Boom De Ay

Stops herself.

I guess that really isn't all that Christmas-y. Hello. I am still the Ghost of Christmas Present. And we're all in the present, aren't we? I hope you are keeping Christmas well. That you remember to be kind and not make it too commercial, but still support our local stores and help them make a living wage. And that you take sustenance from the touching Cratchit family, so happy even though they only have one good meal a year and are extremely poor. Although maybe their lot will improve if I can change this horrid man's character in the course of this evening. Where did you get that Popsicle?

EBENEZER SCROOGE   Someone handed it to me.

GHOST   Bob Cratchit would have given it to one of his children.

EBENEZER SCROOGE   They're about to sit down to an enormous meal. Surely I can have a Popsicle.

GHOST   I suppose. (*to audience*) Now let us watch the Cratchits as they enjoy their Christmas dinner and remember the true meaning of Christmas.

EBENEZER SCROOGE   Why don't you cut your hair off and go buy me something?

GHOST   Be quiet.

The Cratchit family unfreeze around the table. The Ghost and Scrooge stand apart, watching the Cratchits.

THE CHILDREN   Ooooooo, Christmas dinner, Christmas dinner!

TINY TIM   And the goose and the pudding! Oooooh, my little heart may burst.

MRS. BOB CRATCHIT   It looks like a swan. Marthum, is this a swan?

CHILD 2   I don't know. I got it from a lake. I captured it in a big burlap bag, and I beat it senseless with a bat.

LITTLE NELL   A live bat?

CHILD 2   No, a wooden bat.

MRS. BOB CRATCHIT   Well that was very resourceful of you, Marthum.

BOB CRATCHIT   Although normally we like to be kind to animals.

TINY TIM   Just not when we're hungry.

BOB CRATCHIT   That's right, Tiny Tim.

TINY TIM   God bless us, every one!

LITTLE NELL   Father, hurry up and carve the swan, I'm so very hungry. I've only eaten nettles all day.

She holds up little cloth bag that contains nettles.

BOB CRATCHIT   Hmmmmmm, something seems wrong. I can't seem to carve the swan. It's rather tough.

CHILD 2   Did I overcook it?

BOB CRATCHIT   I fear so, Marthum. What little meat was on the swan has been cooked away. There's just skin and bone.

TINY TIM   There's no Christmas goose?

BOB CRATCHIT   Nor Christmas swan neither, it seems.

TINY TIM   Oh. Give me a moment—I must be brave.

CHILD 2   I'm sorry, Mother and Father. I'm sorry, Tiny Tim.

MRS. BOB CRATCHIT   It's inedible. I see. I think we shall no longer call you Marthum. I think we shall call you Useless Child Who Can't Cook.

CHILD 2   Can't I keep the name Marthum?

MRS. BOB CRATCHIT   No you cannot.

BOB CRATCHIT   Darling, Useless Child Who Can't Cook is a very long name. The poor child will be teased ceaselessly in school.

MRS. BOB CRATCHIT   Well maybe she won't go to school. Maybe she'll go straight to the sweatshop like Little Nell.

CHILD 2   Why do you call me "she"? I'm a boy.

MRS. BOB CRATCHIT   Don't tell me what you are. I'll decide, and today I don't know what you are.

CHILD 1   Can I have a name?

MRS. BOB CRATCHIT   No you may not.

TINY TIM   Well at least there's still the Christmas pudding.

THE CRATCHITS (*except Mrs. Bob Cratchit*)   Oooooh, the pudding, the pudding.

Bob Cratchit spoons the pudding out into little dishes and passes them around. The consistency is that of a thick black substance.

BOB CRATCHIT   Ohhhh, it's not overcooked. I can scoop it out.

TINY TIM   Oooooh, the pudding, the pudding!

Bob Cratchit offers some to Mrs. Bob Cratchit.

MRS. BOB CRATCHIT   I'll let you all taste it first.

The Cratchits start to eat the pudding. They make faces, stick out their tongues, put their dishes back on the tray.

THE CRATCHITS   Blllleeeeechhhh! Ehhhhhhyyyyyyyyy!

TINY TIM   It's horrible.

MRS. BOB CRATCHIT   Well of course it's horrible. It's British Christmas pudding. Don't you know what the ingredients are? Rotten fruit and cheap brandy and suet? Don't you know what suet is? It's fat from around animal organs. You think this would make a tasty dish?

TINY TIM   So there's no Christmas dinner, and no Christmas pudding. I can't be brave anymore.

The Cratchit children cry.

MRS. BOB CRATCHIT   This is the very thing I can't stand! All this pathos! It makes me feel hopeless and helpless and I hate it!

EBENEZER SCROOGE   Ghost of Christmas Present, can't we do something?

GHOST   Not without any money.

EBENEZER SCROOGE   I have money. Let me treat them to a Christmas dinner.

GHOST   Really? This is a surprise gesture.

EBENEZER SCROOGE It's so pathetic, it gets on my nerves. And it wouldn't cost that much to feed them.

GHOST Okay.

The Ghost and Scrooge go offstage.

TINY TIM Is there nothing we can eat?

MRS. BOB CRATCHIT Wait a second. I heard something . . . let's wait a moment . . . maybe there will be food.

TINY TIM Oh dare we hope? Dare we?

MRS. BOB CRATCHIT Sure, go ahead.

Scrooge and the Ghost come back, holding many white bags. They also wear little white serving hats. The Cratchits are delighted and amazed.

THE CRATCHITS Ooooooooooh. Aaaaaaaaaah.

LITTLE NELL Look how the pretty white bags float through the air.

TINY TIM It's magic!

GHOST Here you are, everyone. Happy Meals for everybody.

Each of the Cratchits gets a white bag and takes out French fries and wrapped burgers and sodas.

CHILD 1 Oooooh!!! Hamburgers! French fries!

CHILD 2 Ooooh, the French fries smell delicious.

MRS. BOB CRATCHIT Well, the French are known for their cooking.

TINY TIM (*opening his bag*) Oooooh, I have a Big Whopper.

MRS. BOB CRATCHIT Isn't that nice.

TINY TIM Mummy doesn't have a burger.

MRS. BOB CRATCHIT Is there a fish fillet?

TINY TIM   No, just burgers.

MRS. BOB CRATCHIT   All right.

LITTLE NELL   At last it feels like true Christmas now. We have our beautiful tree.

MRS. BOB CRATCHIT   Good God! Who decorated the tree?

TINY TIM   I did.

MRS. BOB CRATCHIT   Are you blind as well as crippled?

LITTLE NELL   Mother, please, I'm saying something positive. Now it feels like a true Christmas. We're all together, and we're happy, and we've exchanged presents, and now we have hamburgers, French fries, and colas. Merry Christmas, everyone.

TINY TIM   Merry Christmas, and God bless us everyone!

GHOST   Phew! See?? That's Christmas in the present, and that's poor people taking joy in little things. I hope it's made an impression.

MRS. BOB CRATCHIT   Well all I can say is . . .

The Ghost zaps Mrs. Bob Cratchit.

Aaaaaaagggghhhhh!

GHOST   I won't have you ruin this happy denouement with one of your sour comments.

MRS. BOB CRATCHIT   All right, all right.

BOB CRATCHIT   Why did you scream, Gladys?

MRS. BOB CRATCHIT   Oh one of those voices . . . never mind. I screamed because I was so happy. (*screams again, to "show" that is how she shows happiness*) Aaaaaaaaaaagggggghhhh!

BOB CRATCHIT   I'm happy too, darling. (*makes mild attempt at "happy" scream*) Aaaaaghh. Merry Christmas, precious Gladys. Merry Christmas, precious children.

CRATCHIT CHILDREN Merry Christmas, Father, Merry Christmas, Mother.

Everyone embraces each other, creating a happy tableau.

"Scene is over" music.

GHOST Now don't anybody move!

The Cratchits stay frozen.

Thank God.

Throughout the next section, the entire Cratchit family stays frozen in tableau.

(*to Scrooge*) So your lesson from Christmas Present is over. Now what's still to come is the scarier visit from the Ghost of Christmas Yet To Come. And I warn you, we'll be going to a very scary cemetery.

EBENEZER SCROOGE Will the Cratchits be part of this? I've really had enough of them. Except for Mrs. Cratchit, of course, I enjoy her.

MRS. BOB CRATCHIT (*pleased*) Oh! How nice.

Note: From now until further notice, the Cratchits from time to time speak while still staying in tableau.

GHOST It's not up to you to say when you'll see the Cratchits again or not. I feel you're forgetting the seriousness of what we're going through. Plus, I have a feeling Tiny Tim may not be long for this world. And Little Nell may die too.

MRS. BOB CRATCHIT Tiny Tim may die? And Little Nell too?

TINY TIM What? This tiny body may be no more?

MRS. BOB CRATCHIT No, pay no attention, children. Mother is writing a book in her head. Pay no attention.

TINY TIM You're writing a book about us being dead?

MRS. BOB CRATCHIT Well, you and Little Nell are so lovable, of course, it would be heartbreaking for a reader to read about you dying.

TINY TIM Oh thank you, Mummy.

EBENEZER SCROOGE Oh God, am I going to have to watch these pathetic children's death scenes?

GHOST Yes, and you're going to like it too.

EBENEZER SCROOGE You mean, enjoy them?

GHOST Oh shut up. Come on, go back to your damn chair, sleep a second, and then the Third Spirit will come. Let's get outta here.

EBENEZER SCROOGE Very well, very well.

The Ghost and Scrooge exit.

MRS. BOB CRATCHIT Don't go!

BOB CRATCHIT Gladys, who are you speaking to?

MRS. BOB CRATCHIT Oh I don't know. I just sensed that those two presences left . . . and well, one of them, you know, seems to like me. His presence cheers me up.

BOB CRATCHIT Whose presence, darling?

MRS. BOB CRATCHIT I don't even know. Never mind. Let's stop standing in this tableau and move around normally, all right?

They break the tableau, and move normally.

BOB CRATCHIT Children, your mother is hearing voices. We must be very kind.

LITTLE NELL I hear voices too. I heard the woman's voice say that Tiny Tim and I are going to die.

TINY TIM Oh dear. And it's true I don't feel very well. I have a feeling I may die.

MRS. BOB CRATCHIT Nonsense. What would you die of?

TINY TIM Of being a cripple.

MRS. BOB CRATCHIT That doesn't make sense. That's like saying you're going to die because you have brown hair.

TINY TIM Nonetheless I feel it. Unless Mr. Scrooge reforms his personality and learns to value Christmas, I can tell I'm going to die.

MRS. BOB CRATCHIT What does Mr. Scrooge have to do with it?

BOB CRATCHIT Oh, Tiny Tim. (*weeps*)

MRS. BOB CRATCHIT He's not dying. He probably feels ill from the Happy Meal, all that fat and grease. Children, if you need to throw up, use one of the white bags the food came in. That's why they put the food in those white bags, it's for vomiting in later on.

TINY TIM No, it's more serious than throwing up, Mummy.

LITTLE NELL I feel my mortality too. I have this little bag of nettles still. What if later tonight, I get hungry again and I choke on one of them?

MRS. BOB CRATCHIT Well you mustn't eat the nettles then.

LITTLE NELL But if I'm hungry . . .

MRS. BOB CRATCHIT Here, give those to me. (*snatches the little cloth bag, full of nettles, that Little Nell has carried from before*) No choking on nettles for you, young lady. I've had enough sickness and pathos, and this stupid family where everything is about suffering.

TINY TIM I think I feel consumption coming on. That's when your little lungs fill up with something and you cough and die, right? (*coughs poignantly*)

BOB CRATCHIT Oh poor Tiny Tim. Other two children, let us pray he doesn't die.

CHILD 1 AND CHILD 2 Don't die, Tiny Tim, don't die!

MRS. BOB CRATCHIT (*to Bob*) Oh why do you encourage him?

LITTLE NELL He's not the only one dying. The spirit said I was going to die. Oh, I think I'm starting to choke on an imaginary nettle.

Little Nell starts to choke. Tiny Tim keeps coughing softly and poignantly. They both continue to cough and choke during the following:

MRS. BOB CRATCHIT Well, if it's imaginary, how can you choke on it? I've had enough. Wallowing in consumption, poverty, no food, no money, this isn't what I signed up for! It seems like I've walked out on you several times already, but one of these times it's gotta work! So long, everybody—I'm going to the pub and then I'm jumping off the bridge. And don't anyone try to stop me. It's a horrible life.

BOB CRATCHIT It's a wonderful life.

MRS. BOB CRATCHIT It isn't!

Music. The set changes to a pub again. The Cratchit family and set somehow disappear.

Scene 10

The pub. A BARTENDER. Mrs. Bob Cratchit comes storming in.

MRS. BOB CRATCHIT Give me a Tequila Surprise, and then point me to the river!

BARTENDER Okay, coming right up.

Mrs. Bob Cratchit chugs her drink down.

MRS. BOB CRATCHIT Mmmm, delicious! Gimme another!

Bartender makes her another. Sound of wind begins. Mrs. Bob Cratchit becomes pushed about by the wind some.

Oh, it's getting windy!

More wind sound, music. Enter the Ghost, dressed in black robes, like the figure of Death. She carries a scythe.

BARTENDER   Oh my God, it's Death.

MRS. BOB CRATCHIT   Finally! Over here, I'm over here!

Ebenezer Scrooge follows the Ghost in, momentarily seeming scared.

GHOST   Ebenezer Scrooge, behold your gravestone!

The Ghost points to the ground. Scrooge looks at the floor, sees nothing.

EBENEZER SCROOGE   Where?

GHOST (*takes off the black hood part of her costume*)   Oh for God's sake. We're not in the cemetery???? Where are we?

Enter GEORGE BAILEY, all happy and hyper. Dressed in a 1940s suit.

GEORGE BAILEY   My mouth's bleeding, Bert! My mouth . . . (*reaches in his pocket*) Zuzu's petals! Zuzu's petals! (*in ecstasy finding the flower petals*) I do exist! Thank you, Clarence. Good old Bedford Falls! It didn't become Pottersville! I've got to go find Mary. Mary, Mary!

He runs off.

EBENEZER SCROOGE   What was that all about?

GHOST   I'm not quite sure.

The sound of a tinkly bell ringing. Enter ZUZU, a little girl.

ZUZU (*in a very sweet, sweet voice*)   Teacher says whenever a bell rings, it's an angel getting its wings.

George Bailey comes back for a minute.

GEORGE BAILEY   That's right, that's right.

George Bailey and Zuzu exit.

MRS. BOB CRATCHIT   I've never heard that.

GHOST   Me neither. Of course, I'm a ghost and not an angel.

Enter CLARENCE, *a sweet, doddering old man of an angel. He has a very large set of wings on his back, making it hard for him to balance.*

CLARENCE   Well it's true. The bell that just rang was for me—I just got my first pair of wings. Saved that man from killing himself. George Bailey of Bailey Savings and Loan. And now I've got these great big things on me. Ooooh, they make me feel a little unsteady. (*to the Ghost*) Hello. I'm Clarence. What's your name?

GHOST   My name is Trophenia.

CLARENCE   Trophenia. What a lovely name. I'm an angel, what about you?

GHOST   I'm a ghost.

MRS. BOB CRATCHIT   I hate all this stuff about ghosts and angels. I don't believe it.

CLARENCE   You don't believe your eyes?

MRS. BOB CRATCHIT   I think you're all a piece of undigested mutton. Or a glob of still fermenting Rice-A-Roni.

EBENEZER SCROOGE   Oh, that's what I said too.

MRS. BOB CRATCHIT   Hello, there. I'm Mrs. Bob Cratchit. Are you Mr. Scrooge?

EBENEZER SCROOGE   Yes. I've enjoyed watching you.

MRS. BOB CRATCHIT (*excited*)   Ooooooh, watching me do what?

GHOST (*notices the flirtation, but focuses back on Clarence*) Clarence, I wonder if maybe you've been sent to help me. I've tried and tried to make Mr. Scrooge reform himself, but this lady, Mrs. Bob Cratchit, keeps getting in the way with all her negativity. And I try to show him his gravestone, and we end up in a pub.

MRS. BOB CRATCHIT Well I'd prefer a pub any day.

EBENEZER SCROOGE Me too.

They smile at each other.

MRS. BOB CRATCHIT Brilliant minds think alike.

CLARENCE Well I love to help people, I'm a very good person. Ummm . . . let me see. (*to Mrs. Bob Cratchit and Scrooge*) Which of you two is Mrs. Bob Cratchit?

MRS. BOB CRATCHIT (*with a look that he's dense*) Well . . . I am.

CLARENCE I understand you have a bad attitude.

MRS. BOB CRATCHIT I have a realistic attitude. I'm living in 1840s London, there's no plumbing, everybody smells all the time, I have twenty children—no, twenty-one—or forty-seven, I don't know!—there's never enough food, my husband earns no money 'cause this man won't pay him anything . . .

EBENEZER SCROOGE Oh, you want me to give him a raise?

MRS. BOB CRATCHIT (*to Scrooge; flirtatious again*) No, you're right, he's not worth a raise. You pay him as little as you want. (*smiles; then back to Clarence*) It's nonstop pathos in my house. The crippled little boy with innocent little eyes. The big galumphing Little Nell, who eats nettles, whatever they are. (*waves the bag of nettles in his face*) And I feel so lonely, and hopeless, and the people around me are icky and goody-goody and pitiful, and I wish I had never been born!

A little ding noise. Clarence looks focused.

CLARENCE Say that again.

MRS. BOB CRATCHIT I wish I had never been born!

The little ding noise again.

CLARENCE Your wish is granted.

MRS. BOB CRATCHIT What?

CLARENCE You got it. You've never been born.

MRS. BOB CRATCHIT Well, nonsense. I'm still here. I'm still holding Little Nell's nettles. (*reaches for the bag; it's gone*) Wait. The bag of nettles, where are they?

CLARENCE You've never been born, so there is no Little Nell. And there's no bag of nettles either. And there is also no Tiny Tim.

GHOST Excuse me. I don't see how this is going to help. Threatening Scrooge with the death of Tiny Tim is a big part of my strategy.

CLARENCE Step at a time. This worked with George Bailey, I think it'll work here too. Mrs. Cratchit, or Person X, since you don't exist, you've been granted a great gift. To see what life would've been like if you hadn't been born. Come let's look and see how your husband Bob would be. (*starts to exit with Mrs. Bob Cratchit; to Ghost:*) We'll be back in a minute, and I bet she'll be a changed woman.

MRS. BOB CRATCHIT Wait a minute. I want Mr. Scrooge to come along, for moral support.

EBENEZER SCROOGE I'd be happy to, fine lady. (*flirtatious*) And you are a fine lady.

GHOST I'm so thrown. Nowhere in the story does Scrooge fall in love with Mrs. Bob Cratchit.

EBENEZER SCROOGE I'm not in love . . . (*with a smile to Mrs. Bob Cratchit*) . . . yet. I'm just flirting.

The Ghost looks a little alarmed by this interest from Scrooge.

CLARENCE Now, now, don't lose faith. Come with me, and

we'll see what would've happened had Gladys Cratchit never been born.

The pub goes away. We're back at the Cratchits' house.

SCENE 11

The Cratchit house. Sad music.

Bob Cratchit is seated, crying, wiping his eye with a handkerchief. Seated on the ground are Child 1 and Child 2.

Mrs. Bob Cratchit, Scrooge, Clarence, and the Ghost are there too, invisible, and they watch.

GHOST Oh, he's crying. Awwwwww.

CHILD 1 Father? Why are you crying?

BOB CRATCHIT It's nothing. (*weeps some more*)

CHILD 1 Are you sad?

BOB CRATCHIT No, children.

CHILD 2 I hope you're not sad, Father.

BOB CRATCHIT It's sweet of you to worry, Little Molly and Little Willie.

MRS. BOB CRATCHIT That's not their names. They didn't have names.

CLARENCE With you not there, they were given names.

MRS. BOB CRATCHIT Well bully for them.

BOB CRATCHIT I'm not crying because I'm sad, children. I'm crying because I'm happy.

CHILD 1 You are?

BOB CRATCHIT Yes, Little Willie.

MRS. BOB CRATCHIT   I would never call a child Little Willie.

BOB CRATCHIT   Sometimes you cry when you're happy because the thing you're happy about has touched a tender place in your heart.

MRS. BOB CRATCHIT   I just hate this man. He's so superior in all his suffering. Does anyone else see it?

EBENEZER SCROOGE   I certainly do.

CHILD 1   Oh, Father, does this mean Mother is bringing home another child?

BOB CRATCHIT   Yes, she's promised she would. Dear Mrs. Cratchit.

MRS. BOB CRATCHIT   I thought I didn't exist.

CLARENCE   Be quiet, please, pay attention.

BOB CRATCHIT   Here she comes now.

Enter Bob Cratchit's wife. Let's call her THE NICE MRS. CRATCHIT. *She's lovely, sweet, calm, generous. She's perfection. She even speaks beautifully.*

She's carrying a little bundle, wrapped up.

THE NICE MRS. CRATCHIT   Hello, Bob, darling. Hello, Little Willie, Little Molly. I have a wonderful surprise for you all.

BOB CRATCHIT   Dare I hope? Is it another child?

THE NICE MRS. CRATCHIT   Yes, I found a foundling on the steps of the church today. Father Meghan M'Golly said he would give it to the Catholic orphanage, but I said, "No, Father, Bob and I so love children, no matter how little money we have, there's always room for another little one."

BOB CRATCHIT   Oh, Mrs. Cratchit. How I love you. You're so wonderful and good.

THE NICE MRS. CRATCHIT And so are you, Bob. The goodness in your heart makes me feel so warm that we don't even need those odd "energy units" you bought from Mr. Scrooge and Kenneth Lay.

BOB CRATCHIT Mr. Scrooge? Who's that?

THE NICE MRS. CRATCHIT Oh I'm sorry. I think he doesn't exist. I mean from your boss, Mr. Lay.

EBENEZER SCROOGE I don't exist either? I don't understand.

GHOST (*to Clarence*) Please, he's the leading character in the work I'm supposed to be doing.

CLARENCE Oh, sorry, I somehow made both of them not exist. How did I do that?

BOB CRATCHIT Yes, Meredith, I'm going to get a lawyer, and look into these energy units. They feel bogus to me.

THE NICE MRS. CRATCHIT Oh Bob, you're so bright as well as loving. Yes, let's go to the law firm of Havisham, Heap and Fagin, and sue the pants off them.

BOB CRATCHIT I will have justice. I won't just lie down and take it.

MRS. BOB CRATCHIT Bob would never say that.

CLARENCE Maybe with you not born he would.

BOB CRATCHIT But I'm forgetting this bundle of joy. Let me look at it. Oh what an adorable child. Hee haw, hee haw. Oh. I felt a sudden pang, of missing the children in the root cellar.

THE NICE MRS. CRATCHIT Now, Bob, we both agreed . . . it was too small for them down there. And we found them a wonderful home, and we didn't have to split them up, Mia Farrow took all eighteen of them.

BOB CRATCHIT Still I do miss them.

THE NICE MRS. CRATCHIT Oh you're so tenderhearted. That's why I love you, Bob Cratchit. But let's focus on the new baby, Hee Haw.

BOB CRATCHIT What?

THE NICE MRS. CRATCHIT Didn't you name the child Hee Haw?

BOB CRATCHIT No, no, I just said that, you know like baby talk. Googie-googie.

THE NICE MRS. CRATCHIT I think Hee Haw is a better name than Googie-googie.

MRS. BOB CRATCHIT Oh she's an idiot.

THE NICE MRS. CRATCHIT Well, we'll name the baby later on. Now, say! Where's Fido? Shouldn't he meet the new addition too?

BOB CRATCHIT Yes, where is that dog? Oh, Fido!

Enter Tiny Tim on all fours, barking and panting.

Look, Fido, a new bundle of joy in the family.

Tiny Tim barks approvingly.

THE NICE MRS. CRATCHIT What a good and loving dog he is. And so good with children.

MRS. BOB CRATCHIT I don't understand, what's this?

CLARENCE Well you weren't born, so the soul of Tiny Tim incarnated into a dog.

MRS. BOB CRATCHIT Really? (*laughs*) I'm oddly amused. Well I don't see him limping. He's not a crippled dog?

THE NICE MRS. CRATCHIT How's Fido's paw today?

BOB CRATCHIT Oh much better. And I taught him to roll over and play dead. Roll over, Fido!

Tiny Tim rolls over.

Very good. Now play dead.

Tiny Tim lies down still.

Good boy. Now, where's Flicka? Oh, Flicka!

Little Nell comes bounding into the room. She is a horse.

LITTLE NELL   Neigh!!!!! Neigh!!!!!!!

She shakes her mane, stomps her foot.

BOB CRATCHIT   Flicka, my friend Flicka—look, a new baby.

LITTLE NELL   Neigh!!!!!

MRS. BOB CRATCHIT   Little Nell is a horse? Well that's fine. Tell me, does she eventually get turned into glue?

THE NICE MRS. CRATCHIT   Bob, I know you love little Flicka. But I've been meaning to speak to you about having her in the house.

NELL/FLICKA *looks mad, snorts, stomps.*

Granted she's a wonderful horse, but she's so big, and she always bumps into the walls and the furniture.

BOB CRATCHIT   I know, Meredith dear. But I feel such a tender feeling in my heart for both Tiny Fido and Little Flicka.

THE NICE MRS. CRATCHIT   Well maybe someday we can afford a stable.

Nell/Flicka doesn't like this conversation, and neighs and whinnies and stamps a bit.

BOB CRATCHIT   There, there, little Flicka, we won't put you in the stable, I promise. Oh Tiny Fido, you can stop playing dead now.

Tiny Tim gets up, pants and barks happily. He now kneels, pants, and does a dog's "begging for food" gesture.

Oh Meredith, darling, I think Tiny Fido and the children are hungry.

THE NICE MRS. CRATCHIT Well, no worry—I have a delicious, elaborate, carefully prepared Christmas dinner simmering in the kitchen. Christmas goose, huckleberries, candied yams, and the pièce de résistance, pudding. And don't worry, children, it's just tapioca—no rotted fruit, no suet, just lovely eggy goodness and those little tapioca things all through it.

CHILDREN Ooooooh, Mummy! Scrumptious!

Tiny Tim and Little Nell/Flicka bark and neigh and show their approval too.

The Nice Mrs. Cratchit exits to the kitchen.

CHILD 2 Oh, Daddy—Mummy is the best mummy in the world.

BOB CRATCHIT Yes, she is, Little Willie. The best mummy and the best wife in all of Christendom. She is perfection.

CLARENCE You see, Mrs. Cratchit—what life would have been like if you had never been born?

Mrs. Bob Cratchit is a bit speechless.

MRS. BOB CRATCHIT Well, yeah. She's perfection, and I was a disaster. So everyone's much happier with me never having been born.

There is a pause.

CLARENCE Well . . . um . . .

EBENEZER SCROOGE She's right. Bob Cratchit seems happier. And he has some energy, and he wants to sue people.

MRS. BOB CRATCHIT And this other Mrs. Cratchit is much nicer than I ever was. They're compatible, they seem to like each other, they both love foundlings. She's a good cook apparently.

CLARENCE Yes, but Tiny Tim and Little Nell . . .

MRS. BOB CRATCHIT Well, Tiny Tim and Little Nell seem happy as a dog and a horse. He doesn't limp, she doesn't work in a sweatshop, she doesn't look like oatmeal as much as she did. They seem fine to me. I mean, I was just going to kill myself, but now I agree with you—I should just never have existed, that's much the better thing.

CLARENCE Yes, but . . .

MRS. BOB CRATCHIT No, let's just leave it as it is—I've never existed.

CLARENCE Well, um . . . uh . . . um . . . uh . . .

GHOST Well, thanks a lot, Clarence! Thanks to you, Mrs. Cratchit is HAPPY not existing; and Mr. Scrooge hasn't learned anything and he somehow doesn't exist.

CLARENCE Now, now, stay calm. Maybe I can get some guidance from Tess or Monica.

GHOST From who?

CLARENCE You don't know Tess and Monica? Have you never been touched by an angel? Used to be on CBS Sunday nights, now you can see it on the Pax Channel?

GHOST I just watch World Wide Wrestling and the Weather Channel.

CLARENCE Well, Monica is the lovely Irish angel, and Tess is the older angel who sings gospel, and each week they solve people's lives in under an hour.

GHOST Do you think Monica and Tess could help us?

CLARENCE Well, Mrs. Cratchit didn't react like George Bailey, so I need help from someone, I'm just this doddering old man with wings. Here, let me try. Tess! Monica! Tess! Monica!

A lovely brunette woman with long hair and a tasteful blouse and skirt shows up on a balcony. We can see her, but the characters can't. I call her LOVELY IRISH VOICE.

An alternate way is to have her only on the sound system. But seeing her is probably better.

LOVELY IRISH VOICE (*with a lovely Irish lilt*) Yes, Clarence?

CLARENCE Oh, Monica. How lovely to hear your lilting voice.

LOVELY IRISH VOICE Thank you, Clarence. Congratulations on your wings. You look fine in them. Tess and I are planning to invite you to a nice vacation in Bermuda to celebrate.

CLARENCE Oh that's very kind of you. Now, the reason I was calling you is . . . well, things worked out fine with George Bailey, but I'm afraid Mrs. Bob Cratchit has decided she likes not existing.

MRS. BOB CRATCHIT I do. I love it. I don't exist, I don't exist! No children, no headaches. I get to sleep 'til noon. Eat bonbons, read mystery novels. It's my kind of life—no life at all.

LOVELY IRISH VOICE Oh, my. Oh heavens to Betsy. What shall we do? Let me confer with Tess a moment. Tess, oh, Tess . . .

Lovely Irish Voice leaves her balcony, or pokes her head offstage. We don't see whom she speaks with, only hear her.

The WOMAN'S VOICE we hear is meant to be Tess, Della Reese on Touched by an Angel. Not looking for an imitation, just a low, melodious voice. And when she speaks, it's an in-the-distance mumble that we can only hear certain words of.

WOMAN'S VOICE (*singing to herself, muffled low voice*)
Amazing grace
How sweet the sound . . .

LOVELY IRISH VOICE Tess, can I confer with you a moment?

The sound of Monica and Tess conferring, in muffled tones, distant. We can't hear what they're saying. We hear the two voices mumble back and forth. Occasionally we hear a word in the midst of the mumbling—probably in the lower timbre of Tess's voice.

LOVELY IRISH VOICE AND TESS'S VOICE (*mostly muffled, we hear occasional word*)   Bzzzz bzzzzz bzzzzz bzzzzzzz God bzzzzzz bzzzzzz bzzzzzzz bzzzzzzz state o' grace bzzzzzzzzzz bzzzzzzzzz bzzzzzzzzz glory be bzzzzzzzzzzz bzzzzzzzzzz.

Everyone listens attentively to this voice.

MRS. BOB CRATCHIT   Gosh, it's turned into a radio play.

LOVELY IRISH VOICE AND TESS'S VOICE   Bzzzzzzzz bzzzzzzzzz heaven bzzzzzzzzzzz bzzzzzzzz Scrooge Mrs. Cratchit bzzzzzz bzzzzzz warm milk.

The conference appears to be over. Lovely Irish Voice returns to her balcony.

LOVELY IRISH VOICE   Clarence, I have good news. Tess and I looked in the heavenly files, and Mrs. Cratchit and Mr. Scrooge are in the wrong century. So you were right to take her out of 1840s London, Mr. Cratchit is meant to be with the second Mrs. Cratchit, not the first.

CLARENCE   And Tiny Tim and Little Nell are meant to be a dog and a pony?

LOVELY IRISH VOICE   Ummmm . . . well I know that doesn't sound right, and we forgot to check on them, but Meredith Cratchit is definitely the correct Mrs. Cratchit. And the Mrs. Cratchit who presently doesn't exist is meant to be married to Mr. Scrooge, and they're meant to live in New York City in 1977.

Mrs. Bob Cratchit and Scrooge look at each other, startled.

CLARENCE   I see. How do we make that happen?

Special spot on Lovely Irish Voice and on Clarence only. Note: Scrooge and Mrs. Bob Cratchit sneak offstage in darkness. Or if seen, exit with a "how very strange this news is" look on their faces.

LOVELY IRISH VOICE Well, let's see. Little Nell the horse should stamp its hoof ten times. Then you and the Ghost of Christmas Yet to Come should say the phrase "Silly Sally sat with Sibyl Setting Spells and Seeking Secret Shadows, Spooks and Specters." You should say it ten times. And then there should be music, lights, and set change.

The Lovely Irish Voice disappears.

In a spotlight Little Nell starts to stamp her hoof ten times, saying "Neigh" on each stamp.

Then Clarence and the Ghost come into a spot and, while Little Nell continues, they intone:

CLARENCE AND GHOST Silly Sally sat with Sibyl Setting Spells and Seeking Secret Shadows, Spooks, and Specters.
Silly Sally sat with Sibyl Setting Spells and Seeking Secret Shadows, Spooks, and Specters.
Silly Sally sat with Sibyl Setting Spells and Seeking Secret Shadows, Spooks, and Specters.

Etc. for ten times; if they have trouble saying it, or get the giggles, that's fine. Less than ten times is fine if set is ready.

SCENE 12

A fancy living room. Modern, nouveau riche furniture, at least a few touches. A big fancy Christmas tree, white, with silver and gold decorations.

Mrs. Bob Cratchit comes into the room, admiring a ring on her hand. She is all dolled up, has a very modern, piled-on-her-head hairdo. She looks good actually.

MRS. BOB CRATCHIT Oh what a beautiful ring. I just love it. 3,455 carats—it's marvelous. Harry, darling—I love it, thank you.

Ebenezer Scrooge comes in, dressed in a fancy satin dressing gown, over slacks and shirt. He uses a walker but otherwise seems fairly healthy.

EBENEZER SCROOGE   What? What did you say?

MRS. BOB CRATCHIT   I said, I love my new present. It's marvelous, Harry. And this is so much better than 1840s London.

EBENEZER SCROOGE   Well, I'm glad you like it, darling. But you called me Harry again.

MRS. BOB CRATCHIT   Ebenezer, dear, I told you, I've changed our names. I don't want to be reminded of whatever that awful other life was. Now your name is Harry, and my name is Leona. And we're the toast of the town, and I eat bonbons all morning, and then in the afternoon I supervise the staff in all your hotels. And, Harry darling, I love my new ring. It's simply marvelous.

EBENEZER SCROOGE   Well I'm glad you like it . . . "Leona." (*twitches slightly*) Bah humbug! Kaplooey! (*back to normal*) Sorry, darling. Just my old Tourette's acting up. Now, Leona, one of our hotels just called up, and said you fired the chief housekeeper.

MRS. BOB CRATCHIT   Yes, I did. I didn't like the way she looked at me.

EBENEZER SCROOGE   How did she look at you?

MRS. BOB CRATCHIT   She looked at me sideways. Like this. (*shows a look, looking sideways, eyes narrowed*)

EBENEZER SCROOGE   Well whatever you think is best. I remember what fun it was to be mean to Bob Cratchit.

MRS. BOB CRATCHIT (*quivers*)   Please don't mention that terrible name to me.

EBENEZER SCROOGE   Well I'm glad you fired the housekeeper and I hope you enjoyed it.

MRS. BOB CRATCHIT   Thank you, I did.

He kisses her.

Don't mess the hair.

EBENEZER SCROOGE I find you so exciting. You're so mean. Do something mean, let me watch.

MRS. BOB CRATCHIT Okay. Serena! Serena!

Enter a downtrodden maid, SERENA.

SERENA Yes, Mrs. Helmsley?

MRS. BOB CRATCHIT Did you finish scrubbing the bathroom?

SERENA Yes. It was hard to get the smell out.

MRS. BOB CRATCHIT Well, Harry's old, what can I say? Serena . . . did you dust in here?

SERENA Oh yes, Mrs. Helmsley.

MRS. BOB CRATCHIT What about the floor?

SERENA I dusted the floor.

MRS. BOB CRATCHIT Did you dust under it?

SERENA Under it? I dusted . . . the floor.

MRS. BOB CRATCHIT I asked if you dusted UNDER it.

SERENA What do you mean?

MRS. BOB CRATCHIT Did you lift up the floorboards and dust UNDER it? Yes or no?

SERENA No. But it would be too heavy to lift up the floorboards.

MRS. BOB CRATCHIT Well maybe I need a maid on steroids who can lift things better. Is that what I should get, Serena?

SERENA I'm sorry, Mrs. Helmsley, wait, let me try to lift up the floorboards now.

She kneels down, tries to lift floor; Scrooge and Mrs. Bob Cratchit enjoy this a lot.

Uhhhhhh. Uhhhhhhh. I think I need a screwdriver.

MRS. BOB CRATCHIT It's too late, Serena. You're fired.

SERENA What?

MRS. BOB CRATCHIT I said you're fired.

SERENA But it's Christmas Eve! I have four children.

MRS. BOB CRATCHIT Christmas means nothing to me. You're fired, get out, get out!

SERENA Oh! It's Christmas, I'm going to starve!

She runs out weeping.

MRS. BOB CRATCHIT You're one of the little people!

EBENEZER SCROOGE Leona, that was delightful. I love you!

MRS. BOB CRATCHIT Thank you, Harry. And I love you, and I love your money and the jewels you give me. Money, status, physical things. That's what I value in life.

EBENEZER SCROOGE That's what I value too. Bah, humbug!

MRS. BOB CRATCHIT Oh Tourette's again?

EBENEZER SCROOGE No, that time I said it for real. Bah humbug on everything except money.

MRS. BOB CRATCHIT Harry, buy me another hotel!

EBENEZER SCROOGE You got it, baby!

Scrooge and Mrs. Bob Cratchit embrace.

Enter the Ghost, now with wings.

GHOST Well, as you see. I got my wings, whatever that means. (*frowns, discombobulated*) So we've gotten Scrooge and Mrs.

Cratchit into the right century. And Bob and the other Mrs. Cratchit are pretty happy back in the 1840s. And so, um . . . (*frowns again*) . . . well the moral of the story confuses me sort of. But there must be one, it all feels sort of right. Let's see. The moral is there are some people who are mean and nasty, but if they enjoy being mean and nasty, then they're happy. That's moral number one. Doesn't sound too good, does it? I bet if I phrased it another way, it would be better. "If you have money, you might as well enjoy it." Maybe that's the moral, I don't know. Moral number two . . .

Bob Cratchit, The Nice Mrs. Cratchit, Tiny Tim the dog, Little Nell the horse, Child 1, and Child 2 come out.

. . . is that there are other people who are very sweet and nice and are just lovely people. And even when they're poor, they're happy. And the mean people can only be happy when they're rich. So the moral is, "If you're poor you can be happy; and if you're mean, you better get money." (*shrugs*) I'm sorry if that doesn't sound uplifting, but the story doesn't make sense to me anymore. Although Clarence and I are about to join Tess and Monica in Bermuda. Maybe after a rest I'll understand it all better. And now . . .

She waves her zapper like a wand; music introduction.

. . . a Christmas blessing from Bob and Meredith Cratchit and their children, dog, and horse.

Ghost moves to the side and watches the Cratchits sing.

BOB AND THE NICE MRS. CRATCHIT (*sing*)
We're so happy and we're poor
Roof may leak but we ignore
All the troubles we may see
'Cause we're filled with gaiety
Hip hooray and yup-de-doo
We feel happy through and through
Though we're poor we have such fun

So God bless us everyone
Fa la la la la la la la!

   Tiny Tim barks happily.

   Enter Scrooge and Mrs. Bob Cratchit.

SCROOGE AND MRS. BOB CRATCHIT (*sing*)
We're so happy 'cause we're rich

MRS. BOB CRATCHIT (*sings*)
I'm short-tempered, I'm a bitch

SCROOGE (*sings*)
Still I love that she's so mean

MRS. BOB CRATCHIT (*sings*)
And his money is quite green

SCROOGE AND MRS. BOB CRATCHIT (*sing*)
Excess wealth is what we love
To succeed you push and shove
So if poor folk fall behind
We can't say we really mind!

   The Ghost comes forward.

GHOST (*sings*)
The moral of the story
Confuses me tonight
Nasty people triumph
No that can't be right

   Enter Clarence.

CLARENCE (*sings*)
The moral of the story
It's best that you be poor
And leave it to the angels
To even up the score

   The Ghost and Clarence zap Scrooge and Mrs. Bob Cratchit.

SCROOGE AND MRS. BOB CRATCHIT   Ow! Ow!

BOB CRATCHIT AND HIS FAMILY (*sing*)
What is Christmas at its core
Giving comfort to the poor

MRS. BOB CRATCHIT (*pointing toward the Cratchits*)
I'm so glad that I'm not there
And I love my brand-new hair

EVERYONE (*sings*)
Merry Christmas whoop-de-doo
We feel happy through and through
Rich man, poor man, said and done
So God bless us everyone

BOB CRATCHIT AND HIS FAMILY (*sing*)
Love your neighbor, help him thrive

MRS. BOB CRATCHIT (*spoken*)   More for me, more for me!

BOB CRATCHIT AND HIS FAMILY (*sing*)
Honest labor, nine to five

MRS. BOB CRATCHIT (*spoken*)   Give me money for nothing,
money for nothing!

BOB CRATCHIT AND HIS FAMILY (*sing*)
And at Christmas please believe

MRS. BOB CRATCHIT (*spoken*)   More diamonds, Harry!

SCROOGE (*spoken*)   All right, sweetie.

BOB CRATCHIT AND HIS FAMILY (*sing*)
Better give than to receive
La, la, la, la, la, la, la (etc.)

 They sing "la la la" under next dialogue.

MRS. BOB CRATCHIT (*spoken*)   Who are these people singing,
Harry?

SCROOGE (*spoken*)   I don't know. I'm going senile.

MRS. BOB CRATCHIT (*spoken*)   Do I have power of attorney?

SCROOGE (*spoken*)   Yes, darling, you get to say yes or no on everything.

MRS. BOB CRATCHIT (*spoken*)   Oh, Ebenezer.

SCROOGE (*spoken*)   Oh, Gladys. Look, I bought you a zillion-dollar tiara. Bah humbug!

MRS. BOB CRATCHIT (*spoken*)   Bah humbug to you too, Harry. (*puts it on*) Oh, Harry. I feel like a queen.

Big musical windup. Everyone does a showbizzy choreographed final verse, with Scrooge and Mrs. Bob Cratchit down front.

EVERYONE (*sings*)
What is Christmas, what's it for?
For the rich or for the poor?
It's for both, you silly Gus
It's for you and me and us

Merry Christmas whoop-de-doo
Though the moral seems askew
Still the tale that has been spun
Ends God bless us every, everyone!

Everyone in their way seems very happy. End of play.